MARKETING CAMPAIGN SECRETS

HOW TO CREATE A MARKETING CAMPAIGN THAT BUILDS POWERFUL BRANDING & DELIVERS GREAT VALUE FOR YOUR CUSTOMERS

TEOH TSE LIANG

Marketing Campaign Secrets

How to Create a Marketing Campaign that Builds Powerful Branding & Delivers Great Value for Your Customers

Copyright © 2020 by Teoh Tse Liang.

All rights reserved. No part of this book may be used or reproduced in any manner whatsoever without written permission except in the case of brief quotations embodied in critical articles or reviews.

Thank you for buying an authorized edition of this book and for complying with copyright laws by not reproducing, scanning, or distributing any part of it in any form without permission. You are supporting writers and their hard work by doing this.

For information contact:

Teoh Tse Liang at www.tseliang.com

Written by Teoh Tse Liang.
Illustrated by Teoh Tse Liang

ISBN: 9798749319033

Printed in the United States of America

First Edition: 12 May 2021

Contents

Acknowledgments 4
Preface. 5
Introduction 8

    Chapter 1.   Branding, Branding, Branding 10

    Chapter 2.   Product, Product, Product. 35

    Chapter 3.   The #1 Question 47

    Chapter 4.   DRS 56

    Chapter 5.   Failure to Launch. 66

    Chapter 6.   99 Problems and Marketing
                          Shouldn't be One. 73

    Chapter 7.   Know your Goals. 91

    Chapter 8.   Strategize Like A Strategist 101

    Chapter 9.   Time for Campaign Planning 108

    Chapter 10. Know your Deliverable. 135

    Chapter 11. The ROAS to Hell is Paved with Good
                          Intentions 140

    Chapter 12. BONUS! 155

Parting Advice from the Author 161
Summary of Concepts 164
Answers. 166
Glossary 183

ACKNOWLEDGMENTS

I would like to thank my wife for running the family in a way that allows me to continue to pursue my passion and my dream. I also would like to thank my godfather for always being supportive of whatever I do and always being a great role model for me in my life.

Preface

All about Tse and His Journey

Hey! It's Tse here. I'm the guy who has been through several war zones and survived when it comes to branding and marketing. I've worked with some of the biggest brands out there - Carlsberg, Somersby, Nivea Men, Magic: The Gathering, Dungeons & Dragons, Transformers – and collaborated with many more. I've spearheaded many campaigns with budgets ranging from as little as $100 all the way up to million-dollar budgets, and generated many more folds in return for the brands that I've worked with. I've experienced many wins and many losses. But I can tell you it's those losses that makes me a better marketer today, not those wins. I've been in the field for over 10 years, and in that time, I've successfully climbed my way up; becoming the Head of Marketing at the age of 32.

So, what's the secret? I got this question from many friends and colleagues. It's really all about the passion in creating marketing campaigns that is impactful for the brand and meaningful for the customers at the end. I've also had the opportunity to work with some of the biggest artists, business professionals, and top-level CEOs; collaborating with well-known media partners and agencies to help me create some of the biggest campaigns ever. And that really gave me a lot of exposure and experience to become a better marketer.

Honestly, the path as a marketer was not an easy one. I've dealt with the dirt, the dust and the drama throughout my journey; learning the best kept secrets behind the scenes on how to create a marketing campaign that builds branding and delivers value to customers – executing, testing, analyzing and optimizing countless marketing campaigns myself. I can tell you I almost burned out along the way, and at one point I could have sworn that I had started to hate my work and I really wanted to give up, but I fought so hard to break through that negative mentality and now I love it more than I ever have. I am really grateful for the decision I made to stay on the path. I still remember it was my first week working in Carlsberg, I thought; "Sh*t. This (I refer to working) is seriously not fun. Totally not what I'm expecting!"

But you know what?

You don't have to go through the "oh sh*t" moments, and you don't have to spend the next 10 years figuring it out.

Why?

Well, because I am going to give it all to you - my experience, my knowledge, my processes - what it really takes to hack it in this game - that I mastered over the last 10 years. Yes, you got it right, all in this book in the palm of your hand. This is my promise. Here's the thing - many people think about the money and the status and whatever glamour first and most of the time those are things that don't matter early in the game. The real deal is - I've called it - The Power 3 - the experience, the knowledge and the processes. If you got none of these, you will not be able to keep the money, the status or the glamour. Even if you do, it will not last, we are not even talking about growing wealth because sustaining it comes first. I can tell you this only because I did not have any of The Power 3 in the early days and I've lost it all - money, business, job.

So, allow me to formally introduce myself.

PREFACE

I'm Tse Liang also known as Tse (pronounced as Z); I am a lover of branding and I love the science behind how marketing campaigns can help to build powerful branding & deliver great value for your customers. And, I am going to share all that from my past 10 years with you in the upcoming 12 chapters!

Are you ready?

Introduction

Have you ever wondered why all of the marketing tactics and strategies that you have tried haven't gotten you the results you want? You're not alone. In this book I'm going to be letting you in on some industry secrets, and my personal formulas to create marketing campaigns that work for any niche and with any budget you have. Now, I'm not here to teach you about Facebook tricks, YouTube hacks or Instagram growth tips, even though I could. No, that is just one small part of the bigger formula. What I'm about to share with you is an evergreen thought process on a bigger scale - a step-by-step blueprint – customized for entrepreneurs and business owners who are running their own business and marketing campaigns. However, this book isn't just for them. If you are planning to start a side hustle, a business or are a leader of an organization, you'll be running a campaign sooner or later inevitably, this is not a book that you will want to miss out on - literally.

Now, before we get started, I want to make it clear that this book is NOT a get rich quick scheme that promises you to make hundreds of thousands of dollars within weeks. This book is also NOT a side business opportunity that you work from home. This book basically teaches everything you need to know about the foundation to create a successful marketing campaign and the process I've used over the last 10 years to create it. It also covers the fundamentals of branding, product, sales and how to prioritize and optimize your goals, strategies and actions. And, I can promise you that once you go through the book, you would have a thought process of a top marketing executive or a marketing director equivalent - equipped with all the knowledge, processes and experience that I collected over the last 10 years and use it to create marketing campaigns for your own business like never before.

Exciting, doesn't it? We've got a lot to cover but don't worry, I am here to walk you through it all. This is going to be a step-by-step guide to a process that I've been using for the last 10 years. It's going to help you achieve and maximize the results that you so desperately want and need for your campaign and your business. Whether your goal is to get more traffic, more sales, or more leads – whatever it is you're trying to grow in terms of your marketing – this is the book for you.

I'll be walking you through some of the most important, most common reasons why campaigns fail. Here's a secret, it is part of the reason why I failed dismally in my early days. At the end of the day, failing to plan – or prepare – and failing to prioritize and optimize will always be the real downfall of any campaign or business, not the fact that they don't know the latest social media hacks and tricks - or how to make a beautiful or a perfect post or video. Remember this, aesthetics can only get you so far. Think about this - if a beautiful post or video was the key, many people would have been successful already but that isn't the case. I'm not saying it is not important, it will increase the chances of people liking it but there are many other factors that contribute to your overall success.

So, if you like what you're reading and getting so far, you're going to like the rest of the book.

I'll see you on the other side!

Chapter 1

Branding, Branding, Branding

① HOW BRANDING WORKS?

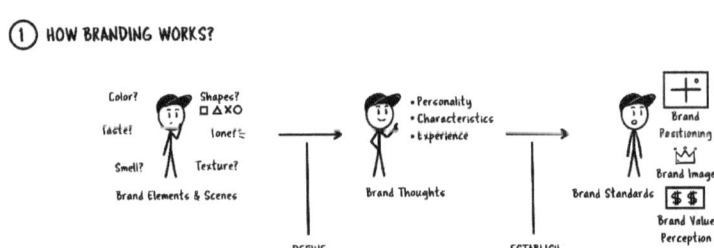

Is your brand helping or hindering your success?

Branding - This is one of the greatest differentiators in marketing - yet one of the most neglected elements for many people who are running their own campaign and business today - especially in this trying pandemic period. Building your brand should always be #1 or one of the highest action items on your priority list. This is the one mechanism of your marketing functions which will allow your customers to really engage with you and your products, or services, on a relatable and highly personable level. In this chapter I am going to cover the 7 key components that will help you build powerful branding and how it plays an important role in making your campaign a success!

Brand Experience

Remember your first date? That impression, that feeling, the whole experience is something you will never forget right? The same happens here. It is about the experience your customers have with your brand. It is very personal. In essence, it is a combination of the thoughts, sensations, reactions and feelings that are aroused within an individual as a result of interacting with your brand. Think about this; what would your customer think or feel when engaging with your brand? What do they think about your brand before engaging your brand and after engaging your brand? Think of it as the lasting impression which your brand has on people. Think about your conversation with your customer. How did your customer feel? Is the tone alright? Is the manner appropriate? The best way to do this is imagine yourself going through your process. How would you feel? Write it down. Go through your 5 senses check. What do you see, smell, hear, think and taste? This impression is vital to brand building as it will last long after their initial encounter with it, and it applies across the board for all niche, industries and markets.

So, what is the actual importance of branding your business?

Firstly, you need to understand that there are tremendous benefits that are derived from positive customer experiences. This in itself can be regarded as an actual marketing strategy; often referred to by seasoned marketers as 'experiential marketing'. You can actually employ a variety of experience-focused marketing campaigns to drive allegiance towards your business and reinforce your brand values, as well as your brand identity.

How awesome is that?!

That being said, you should not confuse user experience with brand experience. They bear a close resemblance, but they are not inextricably linked to one another. They are similar in the sense that they incorporate the exploration of behavioral, cognitive, and sensory responses. However, the user experience is based more on what an individual may take away from a direct interaction with a brand's products or services. Think of user experience as a micro and may vary across channels while a brand experience is a macro and consistent across every channel. Take the following example: Jack browses your website on the phone, went through a seamless checkout process and bought a product, it was a very positive user experience for him; the visual and audio elements on the website and the tone and manner of the copy have delivered a positive brand experience for Jack. All in - the whole experience has totally convinced Jack to make the purchase. Remember this: Experience sells better than products itself.

With that in mind, you should understand that a consistently positive user experience is going to add to a positive brand experience. Ultimately, the user experience impacts the brand experience, just remember they are not one and the same. If you're displaying consistent brand elements as well as a consistent and authentic brand voice throughout, customers will be able to easily recognize and align with your brand over time.

Now, we know why user experience is crucial, but why is brand experience crucial?

It's quite simple. Positive brand experiences will help boost an in-depth connection with your brand, which in turn will deliver the results that you need for both short term and long term. When all is said and done, it is going to be the difference between landing a sale and being overlooked in favor of other brands. Come up with an impressive unique brand experience and you've already won part of the battle - so they say. Deliver it consistently and you will win the war - this is the real secret.

By now, you may be wondering how or what it takes to develop a brand experience that really 'wow' your customers. Not many things in this world can 'wow' a customer for long literally, even if you have something new today, something "new-er" may probably come out the next day or few hours later. However, I am a strong believer in "wow" for brand consistency. For example: The Apple store experience is consistent around the world. That is something worth 'wowing' for. It's no easy feat, but it can be done if you're committed to the process. It all starts with understanding the wants and needs of your target market in depth; in as much specificity as possible through great understanding of the 5 senses. Many entrepreneurs think that they have a really great brand, but they are creating experiences from their own liking instead of the potential customers. You've got to remember you're creating an experience for the customers, not for yourself. While good brands begin in the mind of an entrepreneur, it takes a lot of research, adjustment and preparation to take them from being good, to being great brands that sell like crazy. Many successful brands greatly incorporate the feedback and the needs of the potential users. Let's have a look at some of the ways that you can drive brand presence and loyalty; deliver the ultimate brand experience to your customers:

1. **Event Participation**

Nothing, and I mean absolutely nothing, beats a live, immersive and engaging event. It is the best way to deliver a brand experience to your customers. Participating in events can work wonders at building brand awareness, brand knowledge and brand loyalty amongst customers. Events are one of the best visibility activities a brand can do to increase exposure to the masses. The more visible and exposure you create for your brand, the more likely you are to remain relevant amongst your target audience. Here's what you do - research on past brand events, look at what activities they have, how they engage their audience at the event, and model their successes while creating unique sensory appeal that is identifiable with your brand. It could be a feature of your product that is unique to your product, and your product alone. Play up this 'uniqueness', and use it to your advantage. Since we are here, we may be in pandemic now, but events will be bigger than ever once Covid is over, consumers are eager to go out more than ever, be ready for it.

2. **Engage their Senses**

Buyer behavior is heavily influenced by their 5 senses. Scientifically speaking, in order to grab their attention and hold on to it, you need to be engaging a bare minimum of at least two of these senses. The more the better. Sync their senses to your brand in order to create a symbiotic relationship of sorts, only then will you have created an impactful and memorable brand experience.

3. **Get in on Popular Culture**

Pop-culture is a smorgasbord of opportunities for your brand to connect with your target audience. Timing is everything when it comes to tapping into pop-culture. Think about using a trending meme or social activity to draw attention to your brand. In 2020, the Jerusalema Challenge sparked widespread joy in a tumultuous time. Brands took note of this and soon a variety of entities were doing staff led

Jerusalema Challenges; from small 'mom and pop' eateries to major banks and corporations. There are a few brands, however, that were late to catch the bandwagon, and began posting their own versions of the challenge long after the buzz began to die down. That is a fatal misuse of pop-culture. It will make your brand look irrelevant, and as though your business does not have its finger on the market's pulse. Try to take pop-culture moments and put your own spin on them; in a way which aligns with your brand. If you can pull this off, the results will be powerful.

4. **Make it Personal**

Message personalization is next on our list. Your brand needs to find ways to tell the world its story, in a way that makes it resonate on a personal level with the vast majority of your customers. Make their story, your story and vice versa. Personalization is everything when it comes to brand experience. The reason why online giants such as Google and Facebook do so well is largely due to the fact that the use of the search engine and the app, respectively, leads to a 'tailoring' according to the end user's interests. My news feed and your news feed on Facebook will never be the same, even if we follow similar groups on the platform. The more we use the app, the more tailored to our individual interests it will become. Similarly, our Google suggestions and advertisements that we are exposed to will not be the same. It is possible to tap into personalization to some degree, even if not so in-depth, in order to bring about a high brand experience. Technological advancements such as artificial reality and virtual guidance allow online shoppers to view products in their truest form; giving the end user a real sense of what they're engaging with. Location based services are another way to use algorithm led technology to tailor offerings to your customers according to region. Whichever way you choose to go, the more personalized the experience with your brand, the better.

This brings us to the next important topic. Brand image and positioning. This is going to help you position your brand uniquely with your target market which you've now identified.

Brand Image & Positioning

Brand positioning is the most fundamental, and one of the most critical, components of the broader brand development process. It is incredibly significant in order to explore and refine the level of your uniqueness as perceived by your target audience. Think of brand positioning as a strategy to define the desired position within the mind of your target audience. Think of your target audience looking at a big picture and being able to pinpoint exactly where you are in the image. Before you can attempt to pinpoint your brand position, you need to have a deep thought and a solid long-term strategy behind it. This is going to be your customized stance in terms of engaging with your target audience for a long time. Key components that make up your brand such as your color scheme, shapes, tone, taste and logo must be deliberated on in great detail before going on to this phase. I cannot stress enough the importance of having specific color tones, fonts and graphics that align with your proposed brand image. Let's briefly look at the reasons to give a good amount of attention to brand positioning:

- There are literally thousands, if not more, products that bear a resemblance to yours, which are readily available on the market. You need your brand to stand out, and as such you need to have a good understanding of your target audience's desires, but also of the competition's techniques.
- Being easy to differentiate is going to help you cut through the noise of the market, particularly on the web,

and allow you to engage as authentically as possible with your target audience. What's the one thing that makes you stand out? It can be anything - a personality, a feature or a benefit.

- It is going to allow you to express a perceived value that the target audience will receive as a direct result of engaging with your brand. Irrespective of your target volume, a good digital marketing strategy will allow you to remove doubts from the mind of your target audience.

- Trust is a big one when it comes to brand alignment. Brand positioning gives you the opportunity to gain your target audience's trust by engaging with a clearly visible brand on a personal level. It will allow your potential customers to make quick decisions as to whether or not to choose your brand. Your brand positioning, in this aspect, will act as a mental trigger which draws your potential customer in to making a quick decision on your product or service; thus, driving sales upwards.

- We spoke about the competition very briefly. Not only do you need to know what they are doing in terms of engagement and brand appeal, you also need to know what they're charging. Once you've got a handle on this, you can begin working on your price justification in terms of the product or service that you offer, in relation to the competition. You need to know why your price point may be lower or higher than the competition, and then work on ensuring that this is positively received by your target audience.

- Brand positioning will help you to create a unique visual appeal. Knowing exactly where you plan to fall within your target market, including demographic and geographic details, is going to allow you to craft unique brand visuals and color choices which communicate well with your potential customers.

- In order to create a personalized message and communicate it to your target audience, you need to know exactly where you stand, not only in the eyes of your target audience, but also in correlation to your competition.

These elements will allow you to communicate effectively with your target audience. Once you know where you stand, you can begin thinking about your brand language and tone.

Brand Language & Tone

If you thought brand positioning and having that perfect brand image was important, hold on to your seat for brand language and tone. Brands are so easily accessible in this era, mostly due to the massive accessibility of the internet, and social media in particular. Your brand's voice is what comes across when your target audience engages with your brand; nowadays, primarily via these platforms. Let's discuss the brand voice.

Your brand voice isn't really a voice per se. It doesn't shout out through a device screen. Oh no; instead, the brand voice is part of your brand's personality. Think of a key character like Donald Duck, Elsa or Optimus Prime. The ones that resonated the most with you were the ones whose characters had an impactful voice, weren't they? The language that your brand uses via all avenues of communication is going to dictate how relatable your brand truly is as well as setting a borderline on how they could engage with you and how your brand would engage with them. There will be expectations and we want it to be as clear as possible.

Think about colloquialisms, slang-terms and the like. Is your brand geared towards a more youthful crowd? If it is, such language would be suitable to be employed when engaging with them. Similarly, more formal language would be better suited for a B2B crowd of professionals. You'll need to have a manner of speaking with your target audience, as well as a style and consistent phrase use. Not only should you be using this to communicate with your target audience, it should become a way of speaking to your staff and partners as well. Allow the brand to organically take on a life of its own through its voice. Apply it everywhere; from social media posts to newsletters, and even internal office communications.

But, why does brand voice matter?

If you look and sound like everybody else, you are going to have a difficult time standing out from the crowd. A whopping 70% of the reason why your brand would stand out is due to a unique personality, or voice. You want your target audience to recognize your brand before they even see your name or logo. Use consistent videos, images, graphics and words in order to be recognizable.

How to develop a brand voice

- **Audit yourself**

    Analyze your current communication strategy and find your voice that resonates well with your audience. Sift through old newsletters and social media posts to find out if your brand voice has been clear and consistent. Using different writers and designers to deliver brand messages without having a creative brief in place usually resulted in brand voice inconsistencies. Once you've identified the pitfalls in your communication, look towards top performing posts, most open email headers, most clicked ad, most read blogpost and other means of communication and try to pinpoint what you did right. Moreover, look at what you did that got you good, or even great, responses from your customers.

- **Document it all**

    Document the brand voice and examples of how it has been used before sending this compilation off to various relevant departments that may be responsible for communicating using the brand voice. This is going to come in handy for companies who have multiple departments to become cross-functional to some degree and consistent in employing the brand voice. This is a sure-fire way to keep it fresh, but consistent, in terms of marketing copy across your communication channels. Make sure that at the very top of the agenda on this document, you have highlighted your mission, vision, and values clearly - it acts as a reinforcement and helps most of the time. These should be the starting point for the development of any brand voice. Jot down elements such as recurring words and phrases, hashtags, taglines, and personality traits.

- **Get to grips with your tone**

    While what you say encapsulates your brand voice, how you say it encapsulates your brand tone. That being said, you're not going to be using the same tone for every single avenue. The fun and personable tone that you may be using on a consistent basis via social media is not likely going to be the tone that you use when responding to a customer complaint. In this case, you want to be identifying possible scenarios that would require slightly different tones. Once you've identified these scenarios, segment them into different tones and document possible examples.

If you feel as though you have successfully created a brand voice as well as a brand tone, let's move on to your visuals; brand elements and shapes.

Brand Elements & Shapes

Your brand elements and shapes are made up of tangible facets which represent your brand. They are audio-visual in nature and include signage, letterheads, and promo materials, as well as your tagline, logo and color palette, amongst others. These are the sounds and images that your target audience identifies with your brand. It's a sensory identity which allows them to recognize you immediately. Without further ado, let's take a look at the different types of brand elements:

- **Logo**

    A powerful logo can be so unique and effective that eventually there would be no need for the use of a brand's name on communicative materials. This visual trademark helps identify your brand with specific design elements. Think about logos of brands such as Apple, PlayStation, Starbucks or McDonald's; you would recognize their logos anywhere without having to see their respective names.

- **Brand name**

    This is made up of the words or phrases which are used to recognize your concept, service, or product, as well as your brand's core values. Your brand name shouldn't be off the cuff; in fact, you should take the brand naming process very seriously. Your name is going to tell a piece of your brand story and it is what your target audience will align with for years to come. You want to establish a memorable brand name which will go on to be a household name.

- **Shape**

    Think about the shape of your elements in terms of the shape of your key product or service. Literally take inspiration from the physical product or service which you are aiming to deliver. Relevance is key.

- **Tagline**

    Your tagline needs to have longevity, or staying power. Simply put, you don't want to have to change it frequently.

I bet when I say "Just do it", you automatically know that I'm referring to the sportswear brand, Nike. How about "I'm lovin' it"? Maybe "Because you're worth it" or "It's finger lickin' good"? Taglines help your target audience identify with you.

- **Color**

    The unique 'Pullman brown' of UPS is part of its trademark and easily identifiable. Consumers can instantly recognize any solidified brand merely by its color. This is the reason why 'robin egg blue' was trademarked by Tiffany & Co. in 1998.

- **Graphics**

    These are the symbols, patterns and prints that are found on every single one of your brand's products. A great graphic can help a target audience to identify a brand in mere seconds. Coca-Cola's dynamic ribbon, Coach's unique "C's" pattern, Louis Vuitton's stylized flower pattern, and Burberry's tan and red plaid print are all easily identifiable. Powerful graphics do away with the need to use words; eventually the pattern becomes so synonymous with the brand that it becomes identifiable without even seeing the full picture, so to speak.

- **Movement**

    This can be a bit of an arbitrary element of a brand, and it won't be applied to every single product, let alone a service, but movement can play a vital role in identifying your brand. Scissor doors and their unique up-swing movement are correlated with luxury sports car brands such as Bugatti, Ferrari and Lamborghini.

- **Sound**

    Think about the sound that a Samsung TV makes when you power it on. You know the sound of that brand because it is used for almost all of their devices as a start-up noise and it is further incorporated into their advertisement soundtrack.

- **Taste**

    The unique blend of KFC's 11 herbs and spices is what allows you to differentiate between them and competitor's such as Popeye's. Similarly, a soda lover would be able to tell the difference between Coca Cola and Pepsi.

- **Smell**

    Think about popular perfume brands for a second. If you have a certain preference of scent, you would be able to pick up on its notes almost anywhere. Chanel No. 5's rose-jasmine-musk are trademarked and so are Lush Cosmetics' fresh handmade aromas.

It's quite clear to see that a brand would have particular focus on certain brand elements depending on the nature of its products or services. One thing is for sure; if you're going to get any amount of brand identity and alignment via these tangible elements, you need to take them all into consideration before putting your brand out there. If you're already out there, but are missing some of these crucial elements, you may be at the point where you should consider a rebrand. Rebranding is a huge topic - this is something I will not cover in this book. It is a huge topic on its own.

Brand Color Representation

Color is going to be vital for the success of your brand because it creates the first element that captures the impression for your target audience. Generally speaking, we notice color first, before any other prevailing elements. Your primary colors which can be blended, altered and utilized are red, yellow and blue; although green is also considered a foundational marketing color. Different colors are going to incite different emotional responses within your target audience. Think of a pale blue; it is soothing and calming. Now think about a bright fiery red; it is exciting and reminiscent of danger. Let's have a look at just why color is so crucial.

The psychological inclinations behind color and its impact on human behavior is referred to as 'color psychology'. Not only do we have mental and emotional responses to colors, we may even respond physically, by widening our eyes, standing or sitting up at attention or perspiring ever so slightly. It is mind blowing! No pun intended. Our subconscious mind communicates within itself in color, and it is the reason why color has such a profound impact on our conscious mind.

There are specific colors which have been designated towards specific design groups such as branding, architecture, and interior design. A jaw dropping 90% of consumers will judge a product based on its color scheme alone! Tragic, right?

Competent blue and exciting red revealed consumer's purchasing intent being affected immensely by brand color. Your brand personality will be better identified through your colors and as such, it is incredibly important.

So, what colors can you use for your brand, based on what they represent? Let's find out:

- **Red**

    Red has been known as the color of love, but it is also used to depict power, danger, aggression and intense energy.

- **Blue**

    Blue gives the feeling of serenity, and it incites thoughts of responsibility as well as feelings of trust.

- **Yellow**

    This youthful hue represents optimism and vibrancy. It is an eye-catching color which draws attention in very quickly.

- **Green**

    Lighter shades of this color can have the same impact as blue in terms of feelings of calmness and serenity. Think of green grass and a breeze through lush green trees.

- **Pink**

    Lighter shades invoke a feeling of romance and whimsy while darker shades give off a youthful and energetic feeling.

- **Purple**

    Purple is the color of royalty. Not only is it regal in nature, it makes one think that a product is exclusive and sophisticated. Think about luxury lines of chocolates, lingerie and jewelry.

- **Brown**

    This is a grounding color that asserts dominance. It hearkens to stability and responsibility; generally leading to feelings of trust.

- **Orange**

    This is another youthful color that is often incorporated into brands geared towards children.

- **White**

    When used in contrast with a bolder color, this can invoke feelings of purity and cleanliness.

- **Black**

    Black is another color of sophistication. It demands to be taken seriously and is perfect for the discerning customer.

Just as with your voice and image, you will have to consider some factors before you can begin looking at a color scheme for your brand. Can you imagine using playful colors for a target audience that is mainly made up of business professionals? Yeah, that's not going to go down too well. That being said, let's have a look at some predetermining factors in choosing your brand color palette:

- **Target market**

    Knowing your target market is going to be your first point of departure. Just as you wouldn't simply pick a bright yellow for a brand geared towards a serious legal business, you wouldn't pick black for a brand geared towards children. You have to understand what your core values and offerings are and who your target audience is. For example, if you are creating a color palette for a brand of wellness centers, you might want to consider soothing colors that invoke a feeling of trust and serenity such as blue and green.

- **Appropriateness**

    What message are you trying to get across? Are you loyal to your customers? Are you the best luxury brand on the market? What is it that you want your target audience to think of you? Once you have addressed this, then you can narrow down your color choices.

- **Consistency**

    Once you've picked a color palette for your brand, you need to use it consistently. Use images that predominantly have the same hue as your focal color. Use your colors across all of your marketing materials and communications avenues.

Here's the deal; color is going to be the first thing that your target audience sees before they're close enough to make out your brand name, symbol or tagline. If you're not creating a color palette that is going to be memorable, you're shooting yourself in the foot. Once you've narrowed down your color palette, do some research as to which companies currently bear the same colors as part of their brand. You don't want to come off as too similar to another brand as this could cause confusion, particularly if that brand has a good foothold in whatever market they are operating in. If your brand is geared towards the fast-moving-consumer-goods industry but your color palette is too similar to a brand that is geared towards the healthcare industry, you could find that you have cross-sectional target audiences who could become confused by your use of a well-established brand's colors for something totally different.

Always do your research!

Brand Personality & Characteristics

Have you ever had the misfortune of a bad blind date? Seriously, I want you to think about this for a second. If you've ever had an awkward encounter with someone which left you feeling as though you never wanted to see them again, chances are your personalities didn't match, or they had no discernable personality at all. People engage with personalities. If your brand is flat and has no personality, you're not going to be attracting customers, let alone retaining them. This, just like everything else that relates to your brand, comes down to your target audience. What might be an appealing personality trait for one target audience, won't necessarily be the same for another. Remember this: unique is better than one size fits all.

A truly unique brand will have as much of a unique personality as people do. How your target audience relates to this personality will come down to their preferences and their perceived connection to your brand.

You want to create a personality for your brand that sets you apart from the competition.

Many people think it's hard to differentiate a brand. Now, think about humans in general, we have 7.8 billion people on earth, everyone has a unique fingerprint, can you imagine that? Those lines on your thumb are enough to differentiate you from another 7.8 billion people. Think of how easy it is to differentiate yourself and you will find a way. I'm sure you can easily tell anyone why you are different from another 7.8 billion people without doing a thumbprint check. That's my secret.

Why, is brand personality so important?

Well, people feel more eager to purchase products from brands that they feel a connection with. The connection process will be determined by the following:

- **#1 Relevance**: Does the brand boast a clearly defined image that is relatable and relevant in any combination of the 5 senses?

- **#2 Value > Price**: Is the value more than the price of the products or services and is it appropriate for the target audience?

- **#3 Solve the Problem**: Does the product actually do what it claims to do to solve the problem for the target audience?

Even those who claim to be unphased by brand presence, will be influenced by it to some degree. If it's not a brand that they connect to, they simply won't care about any other factors. This also comes down to perceived value, which we will discuss in the next section. If someone believes that they are getting more value, they will be more inclined to make the purchase. That's all it is.

I'm sure the question on the tip of your tongue is *"How do I improve my brand personality?"* First off, you need to identify, then shape or change, your target audience's personal opinion about your brand. Whether you are strengthening your current brand or developing a new one, you must take personality into account.

If your brand is new to the scene, you're in an excellent position to get off on the right foot with your target audience. Set about developing a personality framework in terms of your product or services, promotional materials, and brand experiences. The best way to do this is describe your 5 senses. The end goal should be for these to fit perfectly within your desired personality. For example:

- Visual - what would I look like if I am a rugged brand? What shapes or symbols will it take? What color will it be? Brown? Dark green?
- Taste - what would I taste like? Earthy? Bitter?
- Smell - what would I smell like if I have a scent? Woody?
- Sound - what would I sound like if I can hear it? Country and casual?
- Touch - what would I feel like I can touch it? Dusty? Rocky?

If you have an existing business, then this process will be a little trickier for you. The basis of your personality development should be centered around analyzing whether or not your target audience's opinions of you match up with your current perception of your brand personality. You could easily use polls or surveys to get more brand insight in that regard. You could find that you're right on the money and that there is very little to change, or you could find that a complete overhaul is required. Make sure you get enough sample size to make a conclusion. I suggest getting at least 500-1000 in order for you to see a clearer picture. Get started!

Brand Value Perception

The perceived value that your customers feel that they receive as a result of interacting with your brand epitomizes your brand value perception. It is the sum total of their experiences, which in turn leads to attitudes and feelings associated with a product or service. This is what gets the sales chart soaring. With the right strategy to create a great brand value perception, you can literally take the most ordinary product and make it the next big thing. Consumers' emotional response to a brand is enhanced with every direct and indirect engagement that they come across.

You can have the best logo, the best brand voice and the best image, but if you can't convince your customers of the value that you offer, you're going nowhere fast. Think of a brand that you have been engaging and seeing for a while but yet to make the trigger. Ask yourself, why is that? What is the gap? Why did you pick another brand and not them? Like why Coco-cola over Pepsi or Pepsi over Coca-Cola? I'm sure one of the 5 senses are more appealing and more valuable to you. Although the consumer is the one who determines this perception, it is your responsibility to align yourself with what they perceive to be of value. This perception is going to be a make-or-break factor for your brand.

Think of your brand value perception as a direct reflection of your product's personality and presence. With this in mind, brand value perception can be achieved via any touchpoints and channels - for example social engagement, public relations, product packaging and even the product development phase itself. Many world-renown watchmaker brands like Rolex and Audemars Piguet use the process of watchmaking craftsmanship to uniquely establish their brand identity and expertise. And because of that, admirers and customers are convinced of the greater value of the craftsmanship and willing to pay the price tag undiscounted plus tips sometimes. They totally believed they were getting something of significant value compared to the price tag. If you can get all of this right, you'll have a naturally winning product in terms of your target market's perception of its value.

But why is it so important?

It is going to be a direct reflection of your target audience's opinion of your company culture. It's incredibly important to get this right the very first time because the longer that a target audience has one perception of your brand, the harder it will be to change that perception to something else. This is equally true for negative and positive perceptions, which is why businesses that get a good brand value perception early on, often rise above certain challenges as the years go by because that perception amongst their target market drives great following and great loyalty.

Now that's great and all, but I'm sure you would like me to get to how you can measure your own brand perception. Just remember - this is a long-term investment for your business. It may take years to go to where you really want to be. The goal is stay consistent and keep going. You could try any of the following methods to find out your brand value perception:

- Track online mentions by establishing Google alerts;
- Go through online reviews, and find out where your key challenges lie from the eyes of the consumer;
- Measure metrics for pay-per-click dwell time;
- Use social listening techniques including the analysis of hashtags, social media comments and other mentions of your brand;
- Utilize custom research amongst secondary and primary target audiences;
- Track metrics within the target audience surrounding your brand;
- Track consumer sentiments throughout every purchase stage. This should include information search, comparison research, product evaluation, purchase decisions as well as post-buying emotions; and last but not least,

- You should conduct a brand audit on brand perception against leading competitors.

You need to be constantly measuring your brand perception from the outside in on a consistent time frame. Yes, as marketers, entrepreneurs and business owners, we tend to get deeply attached to our brand. However, you are doing yourself and your brand an immense disservice if you are not seeking to understand your brand from the perception of your target audience. Remember, your branding is your advantage! The more unique and clear you are about yourself, the more outstanding you will be.

CHAPTER 1: RECAP
Exercise That Mental Muscle

1. What is your Brand Experience'?

   _____

   _____

2. Why is brand experience important?

   _____

   _____

3. List the 4 basic ways that that you can drive your brand presence.

   _____

   _____

4. What is the importance of Brand Image & Positioning?

   _____

   _____

5. What is your brand personality?

   _____

   _____

6. Why does brand voice matter?

   _____

   _____

MARKETING CAMPAIGN SECRETS

7. List the 3 basic ways to develop your brand voice.

_____

_____

8. What are the 10 basic brand elements?

_____

_____

9. What percentage of consumers judge a brand based on its color palette alone?

_____

_____

10. What are the predetermining factors in choosing a brand color palette?

_____

_____

11. What is the first stop on your list in terms of improving brand personality?

_____

_____

12. What is Brand Value Perception?

_____

_____

13. Why is brand value perception important?

_____

_____

Give it your best, and head to the end for the answers.

Chapter 2:

Product, Product, Product

② HOW A PRODUCT CAN WIN?

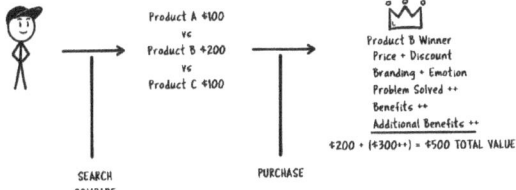

What are you selling and offering?

When it comes to selling, anyone can set up an online shop and sell just about anything right this very minute. The difference between products that just sell, and products that sell like hot cakes is your USP; or unique selling point. Whether you have a service, online program, consultation - I categorize them all under "Product" in this chapter. Let's continue:

What makes your product different from the rest?

What is it that you are offering that is different, what value are you giving to your customer through your product? What exactly are they getting?

I want you to think about this very seriously. We are moving further into a digital age; where products are available at the click of a button. Not happy with your current service provider? There are literally hundreds more; all lined up and waiting for you to take your pick. Many are willing to go very low price and even more are willing to go free. This makes your 'uniqueness' incredibly crucial for the survival of your business.

I don't want you to focus on success just yet; I want you to focus on surviving your early years. Did you know that more than 60% of new businesses fail within their first 5 years of operation?

60%! That's close to two thirds of all startups.

I'll tell you what I've discovered to be the Achilles heel amongst almost all of these businesses; unrealistic expectations.

Sure, I want you to shoot for the moon; I want you to have success in mind, but not to the detriment of your business' survival. You can't put the cart before the horse. There is a process to achieving success; and most of the so-called overnight success stories you've heard of have actually been years in the making before catching the public eye. In order to walk, you first need to crawl. In order to succeed, you first need to survive these first few uncertain years.

I need you to grasp this concept so wholeheartedly that the very notion of success is correlated to survival in your mind. It's not going to be an easy process; nothing that is worth it ever is. You need to re-program yourself in order to adopt a mindset whereby hard work is the only way forward. With grit and focus you can move your business from surviving to thriving.

Whether you're an entrepreneur, a business owner, a freelancer, whatever title you possess that requires you to sell yourself, your services or your products; you are going to have to come to the realization that you need to knuckle down and push through some of the most exhausting work days of your life. Starting a business is not all roses and cocktail hour meetings; it's extremely hard work that requires you to commit more of your time than you would do in your average 9 to 5. Just as your brand has to be representative of the people whom you are selling to, your business ethic has to be the same. You work for the masses, not for yourself, and you work on their schedule with their needs in mind. If you think owning a business means that you'll have more time to kick back and relax, then you are sorely mistaken. Yes, it will give you the financial freedom and with that, the freedom of your time that you have envisioned, but that is not going to be the case straight out of the gate. That is the end result if you succeed.

Why?

Firstly, you must have an offer, then you must be able to sell your offer to customers, then you think about how to hire people and grow your business. Finding key personnel whom you can entrust with the growth of your business will undoubtedly lead to more freedom of your time, because with time you will be able to trust them enough to delegate high level tasks. The reason why I emphasize this early stage of your business so much under this section is that you need to know exactly what you are selling in order to sell it, and sell it well. You are going to be going through a lot of uncertainty in the early years. Effectively, you'll be learning to fly as you build the aircraft around you. Your brand vision, personality and tone will take shape during this stage as you adapt to incoming information from your target market.

The most important part of this period is going to hinge on your ability to sell. If you don't have the ability to sell, you are not going to survive in a highly competitive market. It's as simple as that. You would be better off sitting it out and not even attempting to start your own business if selling is not for you. If the mere thought of engaging with your target audience on a very real and authentic level puts you off, or makes you feel uncomfortable, well I've got news for you; you'll be going nowhere, fast.

Now that I've got your attention, let's get to work on providing you with the tools to be an expert seller. I'm going to use some simple tips to help you apply my years of industry-based knowledge to your own business.

Sound good?

Great! Let's rock on.

The set of questions below are going to be your first step towards building a stronger survival kit and it revolves entirely around your product and how to sell it. Try to answer these questions:

1. What is your product?
2. What exactly does your product do?
3. What problem does your product solve?
4. What are the features and benefits of your product?
5. Can people live without it?
6. Why should people buy it?
7. Are there any other similar products in the market?
8. If yes, how much do each of those products cost?

9. Can this problem be solved by using any other means aside from using your product or the other similar products?
10. If yes, what is it and how much does it cost?
11. How much are you pricing your product?
12. Why is it priced at this amount?
13. Would people pick up your product over all other products or other means?

Try using a table similar to the one below in order to benchmark your product or service, before coming back to the questions:

	My Product/ Service	Competitor 1	Competitor 2	Competitor 3	Comparative Product / Service 1	Comparative Product / Service 2	Comparative Product / Service 3
Price							
Problem it Solves							
Benefits							
Can people live without it?							
Reasons to believe / purchase							

Do you rank favorably in comparison to your competition? Do you rank favorably in comparison to comparative products that could work in place of your product? Think of the latter as substitutes instead of direct competition. Now, grab a pen and paper, let's go back to those questions.

What is your product?

This one is pretty straight forward. At the very least, you should know what your product is. I mean the whole kit and kaboodle. Know every intricate detail of the product, down to the type of material the screws are made out of; if it's a physical product of that nature. There should be no one that knows your product better than you. When you know your product with absolute clarity, you'll be more confident in terms of how you sell it.

What exactly does your product do?

What purpose does your product serve? It's not enough to know the product, you have to know what role it fills and how that role is going to be perceived by your target market. Read the question again and write down the one-line statement for your product. Whether it helps you to slim down, save power, eat more, eat less, make more money - add numerical - in 10 days, in 1 week, in less than 24 hours - add barrier - without exercise, without sacrificing carbs, without cables. Example: Product A can help you slim down in less than 7 days without you exercising at all.

What problem does your product solve?

If you're not solving a problem, or filling a need, do you even have a leg to stand on? The answer is simply, no. Don't fumble through this step. Gauge whether or not your product or service will be solving the problem you promise to solve. More importantly, is the problem far reaching enough to create the sales numbers that you need in order to take your business from surviving to thriving?

What are the features and benefits of your product?

Once you've determined the problem that your product or service solves, you need to get specific about the features of the product and the benefits of using the product. Many people neglect the features but some products rely heavily on features especially if you are talking about machinery, tech, electronic devices. Make sure you list them out clearly in detail. Obviously, and primarily, the paramount benefit is the solution to the aforementioned problem, but what other subsidiary benefits come about as a result of using your product?

Can people live without it?

We can't all create products that people can't live without. If we all worked towards only creating products that were a necessity, there would be no donuts, toys, or other fun creations. While the goal is to create something that people 'feel' that they cannot live without, you can place equal importance on creating the perception that they cannot live without your product or service. Showcase how the use of your product or service will benefit their lives in such a revolutionized manner that they begin to *feel* as though they cannot live without it. It's all about emoting.

Why should people buy it?

So, you think you know the problem that your product solves as well as the benefits; you may even have a proposition as to why people can't live without it. You're going to have to bundle all of this up into one airtight package, no pun intended, and put a spin on why people should buy it. What is the key, defining element that would make people want to rush out and get it today? Focus on the value you are giving to your customers and convince them you are giving more than any other product. The idea is to have one standout element - so that you can shout about it. Make sure that element matters in decision making.

Are there any other similar products in the market?

This one is given. Of course, there are going to be similar products in the market. Identify them and plot them into a benchmark table, such as the one above. Remember this: Customers always compare - unconsciously - and all customers prefer to get more value than less. That 2mg of extra calcium is what many parents look at when buying cheese for their kids. Do your groundwork. It will come handy for you in the long run.

If yes, how much do each of those products cost?

Consider how much each of these products costs. No, you don't have to make a list of every single competitor in your market; just peg the most important ones. In other words, benchmark the top 3 who have a large market share.

Can this problem be solved by using any other means aside from using your product or the other similar products?

Now this is where it gets a little tricky. Think about bottled soda and bottled water. They both fall into the beverages category but one falls into the soft drink subcategory while the other falls into the bottled water subcategory. These are comparative products, as opposed to competitive products. A comparative product is one that your customers, or potential customers, would pick as a substitute for your product. Seemingly, bottled water has more benefits than soda, in terms of health benefits, and would thus be a better choice by comparison.

If yes, what is it and how much does it cost?

Identify the comparative products that may or may not fall into the broader spectrum of your category and look very closely at their prices. If the comparative product is more beneficial than your product, and cheaper, you're not going to stand a chance against them.

How much are you pricing your product?

This is the tricky part – you've got to evaluate and factor in all the branding aspects we have gone through in Chapter 1. There are other elements that you should consider like how many years of expertise, how long has your brand presence in the market, awards won, etc. Make sure to incorporate all that, but if you are fairly new, with no reputation or other success as a convincing point, premium pricing is not likely to work unless you are the only one providing that product to solve a very big issue. Then you have struck a goldmine. Be competitive. Focus on your long-term success and make reasonable short-term gains. Sometimes, a little sacrifice upfront can give you big gains for a long time.

Why is it priced at this amount?

More often than not, there will be something trivial that is making your product more expensive than that of the comparative or competitive products. Look at everything from your warehousing costs to unnecessary package design 'frills' which are not necessarily helping you generate sales. Cut back anything that is not immediately important in order to give your pricing the competitive edge.

Would people pick up your product over all other products or other means?

Finally, get real with yourself. There is absolutely no point in blowing smoke up your own backyard in an attempt to save your ego. Look at your product from the outside in, and if necessary, set up a test panel to test your product against the competitive and comparative products which you've now defined. You want to get down to whether or not your product would be picked over all the others, and if not, you need to know the reasons why so that you can address this.

Ultimately, you need to know your product with intricate detail. Not only should you know your product, you should know the environment in which your product fits in. Think about how many millions of products are listed on the Internet, Amazon, eBay, Facebook Marketplace, Shopify, and any other private selling platform. A world of products and services are available with just a few swipes, scrolls or clicks.

If your product does not come across as something that serves a distinct purpose as well as something that is going to have longevity, then you're not going to be doing very well when it comes to selling your brand and its products.

Remember that this first phase of your business is all about weathering the storm. You need to be able to absorb information as quickly as possible in order to translate it into meaningful changes which can be applied across the board, not only in your sales efforts, but in your business growth and branding efforts.

Adaptability is crucial. Remember this: Emotion is a bad multiplier in an equation. Make sure that you're objective about your product and your business at all times and focus on serving up great value and great quality that will make the target market say, "How on earth did we live without this before?!"

CHAPTER 2: RECAP
Exercise That Mental Muscle

1. What helps products to sell like hot cakes?

   _____

   _____

2. What percentage of new businesses fail within their first 5 years of operation?

   _____

   _____

3. What do you need to focus on in your early years?

   _____

   _____

4. List the questions that you need to ask yourself in order to benchmark your brand against the competition?

   _____

   _____

5. What are the products called that serve as substitutes instead of competition to your brand?

   _____

   _____

   Give it your best, and head to the end for the answers.

Chapter 3:

The #1 Question

How do I increase my sales revenues?

I get this question a lot. It is the #1 question that I get asked on a regular basis, and understandably so. We are all trying to find ways to increase revenue. Whether you are working on your business or working for someone else - this is the #1 question of all time. Increased revenue comes from an increase in sales. The great news is, if you've paid attention to the previous two chapters, you are well on your way to increasing your sales.

Although diversifying your outputs is a great way to increase revenue, if your current customers are not being satisfied, no amount of diversification is going to help you. Your first port of call will be to pay attention to your existing customers. If you already have some semblance of market share, you will want to solidify your relationship with them before trying to win any more clients over to your side. Word of mouth is more important now than it ever was. I'll keep driving home the fact that we live in a digital age. People could be reviewing your products or services without you even knowing about it; but you should know about it. Just a simple search on the net and on social media networks can give you insight into what people are thinking and saying about your offerings. If you do come across a bit of negative feedback, it's important to take it into consideration. This is going to help you to understand where you may be going wrong from the customer's perspective. It's also a great way to tap into some positive feedback and build on it. Find out whether or not this feedback has anything to do with the branding concepts as well as the selling concepts we discussed in the first two chapters. You may very well find that you're missing the mark on something incredibly simple which can be addressed just by following the previous steps.

You want your customers to feel as though they're part of the family; giving them specials, rewards and benefits that newer customers may not have the opportunity to tap into. It's important not to alienate newcomers, but to make your patrons feel appreciated, heard and acknowledged. Social media pages are a great way to accomplish this, but remember, you want the communication stream to be as authentic as possible. Make it personal and direct your efforts, and perhaps additional funding, towards customer service and client retention. When you've got a good group of existing customers who are raving about what you have to offer, it's easy for your page, and thus your products, to go viral. Then it's "hello, sales!"

Once you've managed to find a way to appease your current customers, you will want to shift your focus to innovating in your category. This ties really closely to the subject of filling a need, or solving a problem, as we discussed earlier. If you have even a shred of negative feedback, it could actually do a world of good for you.

How so?

Well, for starters, you wouldn't have to look very far to find a problem to solve; it could be right on your front doorstep. Not only do you want to be projecting an image of being better than the competition, which we will discuss in this chapter too, you want to project an image of being better than you once were. Instead of trying to sweep your problems under the rug, give them the spotlight and highlight how you've gone about solving these problems for your existing customers. It will give your brand an air of transparency, and build the trust upon which sales are grown. Do it in a fun and candid way and you'll have your customers laughing all the way to your purchase section; while you'll be laughing all the way to the bank.

This is another fantastic way to grow the perception of the value which you bring to your customers. As I've already mentioned, there could be thousands of products which are similar to yours, but if you're constantly working towards resolving your customer's problems and providing value added services, you are going to come up as being a cut above the rest of the competition. Everything is so fast paced these days; fast food, fast shopping, fast internet. You should be focused on making the customer experience as fast and efficient as possible, but do not confuse this with the speed with which you should attend to clients. Focus on answering their questions and attending to their concerns quickly, but don't be so focused on speed that you try to rush through servicing their needs. Take the time to truly appreciate their concerns and train your customer service personnel to only close off communication once the customer is well and truly satisfied with the product or service. Go the extra mile and institute 'after-contact' communiques; taking the initiative to reach out to the client even after they claim their concern has been satisfied. This way your customers will always feel connected to you and as though you truly care about them. In the year of the global pandemic, so many ties were severed or weakened due to the isolating effects that social distancing and the subsequent lock downs imposed on us all. People are craving genuine connection now more than ever. If you can tap into that, you may have struck gold.

If you're going to be getting into social media, and subsequent online advertisements such as sponsored and paid advertisements, then you need to know something before you go about doing that. Ads drive sales, they always have; whether in print or electronic format, adverts can drive your sales through the roof. However, it's not enough to have advertisements with fantastic imagery and brilliant sales copy, if you do not have a clear call to action, you're literally pouring money down the drain. I've come across so many sponsored posts on social media that are seemingly catchy but are heavy on text and not straight to the point. You've only got about 3-7 seconds to grab someone's attention and stop them in their tracks as they scroll through their news feed. So, make sure you have an attention-grabbing headline, you've got that 3-7 second window to make an impression. Draw your audience in; but just be sure that what you're offering actually lives up to the headline. Once you've got them reeled in, direct them straight towards a sales page or a sales funnel; essentially somewhere that they'll be able to get all of the juicier details on what you're offering including how to make a purchase. Make sure you cover all the essential details and values you are giving in your sales page, refer back to Chapter 2.

Now, there's a reason why the checkout counter is lined with a bunch of goodies that we may not have had on our shopping list in the first place; this follows the principle that if you place something that seems like a great deal close enough to a checkout spot, customers are more likely to make what is known as an 'impulse buy'. Make sure to have the upsell element at the checkout area of your sales page. This mechanism has a great 10-30% conversion rate depending on how relevant the upsell product is. Example: People who bought a leather shoe are likely to buy a leather care ointment for their shoes or people who bought a dumbbell set are likely to buy a workout bench. Get the concept and implement it on your sales page.

Another way to drive your sales up is to give limited time offers or a 'money back guarantee'. Do you know what this does for your target market? It removes the element of risk from their minds. Many of us are feeling the financial pinch lately so taking a risk on a new product is going to be the last to-do item on our lists. If you're confident enough in your product, and honestly you should be if you're planning to retain any number of clients, then try out limited-time, money-back guarantee offers. Make sure to include terms and conditions that are going to protect you from the chancers out there. Yes, unfortunately there are people who just want to spoil the fun for all of us, so be sure that you've got your legal ducks in a row to avoid having to shell out for people that seek to take advantage of the deal you're offering. Once you've safeguarded yourself against such people, go ahead and roll the deal out and watch how your sales numbers grow.

This brings me to my next tactic as part of promotions which we will discuss in broader detail under Chapter 6. Having credible people review your product or service can do wonders for your business. Restaurants and hotels have been doing it for decades. Pick up on someone notable with an interest in your product category, then offer them free merchandise as a way to promote your business. Not everyone will be able to afford the promotional fees of the likes of Kim Kardashian, but you can find influencers that are within your financial reach. Bear in mind that a lot of people buy followers nowadays, so look towards page engagement. If you find someone on Instagram whom you think has a good enough following to promote your brand, have a look at how many comments and likes they have on their posts. Someone with 200k+ followers who only averages 100 likes and a handful of comments most likely purchased those followers. In the end, you'll be sending them free merchandise with next to zero exposure for your product; or worse, you may have even paid them a fee to do so. At the end of the day, make sure you do your research on any and all potential partners, and supposed influencers.

Testing, testing, can you hear me? Testing is going to be the final way in which you can grow your sales. We discussed this in the previous chapter and I would like to focus on it a bit more at this juncture. The feedback that you get by testing your product is so vital to your success. Whether you are launching a new product or just trying to see if your product is still relevant in the current market, testing is the best way to do this and it will always be money well spent. You need to take an introspective approach to selling in this regard. What are you doing right and what are you doing wrong? What can you build on what you are doing right, and how can you fix what you are doing wrong? Get your product in front of people who aren't going to pull any punches. If you are not well versed in conducting test research, don't waste your time and money attempting to do it yourself. There are experts in this field for a reason; they know exactly what questions to ask in order to get the most impartial and accurate responses. We tend to lead people with questions in the hopes to get out of them what we want to hear. This is not going to help you in the least bit. Think about typing a question into Google. If you type in "Is testing good for sales." Google is going to sift through information to give you a majority of answers in favor of the question, and it will do the very same thing, giving you the opposite answers if you type "Is testing bad for sales" into the search bar as well. These are leading questions, and leading questions get led answers; but this is just one type of example of where it could go wrong for you if you were to try and conduct testing completely on your own with no prior experience. Although it's not impossible, it may end in failure; thus, delaying the results that you need in order to drive your sales. You need objective questions in order to get fair and objective answers.

So, remember, retention over attraction. Keep checking in with your existing customers to make sure that they are in fact satisfied with what you're offering. Test your product over and over again to make sure that you're still relevant, and never ever advertise without some sort of promotion attached to it. Word of mouth is still relevant in this day and age, if not more so than before. People are constantly typing away; letting the world know what they think of every single thing that they come across. Everyone's got an opinion, and everyone either wants their 5 seconds or fame or wants to feel as though they've done their good deed for the day by telling people where and where not to spend their hard-earned cash; it's the reason why review sites are still so popular and why Facebook, Amazon, eBay, or just about any site with ecommerce capabilities, have a review option for product pages. Make sure you're on the good side of those reviews, and when you find that you aren't, don't try to sweep it under the rug. Showcase to your clients; past, present and future, that you have what it takes to make amends when you've gone awry. Trust and connection are everything, and this is the end game you want to build.

CHAPTER 3: RECAP
Exercise That Mental Muscle

1. What is the number 1 question I get asked on a regular basis?

   _____

   _____

2. Is diversification going to help you if your current customers are dissatisfied?

   _____

   _____

3. How do you make patron customers feel special?

   _____

   _____

4. Should you alienate newcomer customers in favor of patrons?

   _____

   _____

5. Is negative online feedback bad or good, and why?

   _____

   _____

6. Should you try to speed up the communication process when you're resolving a customer service issue?

7. How do you go the extra mile after you've been in contact with a customer?

8. Can you release sponsored posts without a call to action?

9. How many seconds do you have to stop people in their tracks as they are scrolling?

10. How do you safeguard yourself from chancers in terms of money back guarantees?

11. Are reviews bad or good for public image?

12. Can you conduct product or service testing on your own, and why?

Give it your best, and head to the end for the answers.

Chapter 4:

DRS

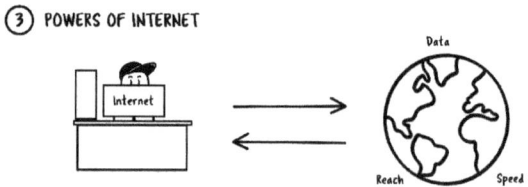

Hint: It's not just Formula 1 Cars.

We've spoken quite a bit about how the internet has shaped how we interact with our target market. This is because it is so incredibly true. It is also quite difficult to market a product to a target market now because there is so much noise that has been created by 'fly-by-night' would-be businesses that are trying to cash in on the internet's gargantuan pool. Just because the internet seems like a more cost-effective way to market your products to the public, don't be fooled into thinking that you can get it done for next-to-no cost. On the contrary, online marketing is still going to cost you. In order to make more money, you need to spend some money. Look at how much money Elon Musk, Bill Gates or any CEO invested in learning, development, research and marketing for themselves and their company. Model what successful people do and not what others are trying to do. Learn the secrets that make them successful. Many people stopped here because they think they cannot be Bill Gates. The thing is everyone can be like Bill Gates - you can learn to think like him, plan like him, have great vision like him - you just got to invest to learn and be better. The same principle applies here for marketing. You've got to invest; you've got to spend in order to grow and make more money. I'll discuss the principle of making your money work for you more in Chapters 11 and 12.

Although it will definitely cost you to get a business off the ground, or to grow one from surviving to thriving, there are some incredible capabilities that the internet has granted us with which can help us get to our goals a little faster, and more affordably, than traditional methods. Have you ever heard of the term DRS? DRS refers to the Drag Reduction System that is in place in newer Formula 1 cars in order to increase their speeds for takeovers. I want to use this concept to show you what's the DRS in the internet - in order for you to increase the speed with which you reach your target market and drive your sales. DRS for you would refer to as Data, Reach, and Speed. Remember that from now.

Nowadays, at just a fraction of the cost, and with a device that lies right in the palm of your hand, you can reach out to just about anyone across the globe. How incredible is that? Think about the resources that had to be utilized in the past to sell products; I'm talking about way before the advent of the internet and what it has evolved into today. The sheer volume of financial and physical resources that would need to be in place to sell just one line item is jaw dropping. Now, one might argue that the internet has done more harm than good in the sense that the corner shop is no longer just battling with competition in the neighborhood but also with competition from the furthest recesses of the globe. Fair enough, but if you evolve your thinking and your strategies to meet this challenge, you can achieve supersonic revenue levels.

Let's get back to the notion of a sales DRS system. Just as the traditional sense of the term gives Formula 1 cars the ability to overtake rival drivers, your DRS system can give you the ability to conduct your sales initiatives at a far greater rate and capacity, thus sling-shooting you around and ahead of the competition. The only real cost that you would have to contend with on a consistent basis is the cost of a good internet subscription; taking into account that you already have the correct human resources in place to help you drive your sales. This, of course, is dependent on the scale of your business goals.

The internet is a massive place. It is another world and another realm of almost infinite possibilities. All that it requires of you is to see it for what it is and to engage with it from a positive mindset. Look, I know a lot of you may feel a bit overwhelmed when it comes to utilizing the internet for your marketing efforts. I've had a lot of people say that they don't even know where to begin, but it's an easy formula to learn.

Why?

Well, for starters, numbers don't lie. Figuring out a method to utilize the calculable algorithm is a lot easier than you think; it's all sequencing and numbers after all. This DRS approach is a sure-fire way to ensure that you maximize on the algorithm and work with it, instead of against it. Many popular advertising platforms such as Facebook and Google have great tools and dashboards that are literally ready and set up for you. All you need to do is learn how to read the metrics, rearrange the column and connect the dots to tell a story.

If you can successfully line up your data with your reach and roll it out in a fast enough manner, you are going to be able to unlock 3 groundbreaking benefits that will have you asking yourself why you couldn't see the simplicity of it all along. Firstly, it will take the limits off of your possibilities for achievement. With unlimited reach comes unlimited possibilities. Secondly, you're going to find that there is an abundance of resources at your fingertips. Yes, you heard that correctly. There are thousands of platforms, programs and applications that can take your marketing approach from mediocre to mega-bucks in no time. Here's the kicker; some of them are actually free. Now, I could literally take up the next hundred pages just to list some of these out, but that's not what this reading journey is about for you. I'm here to hand you the tools, but you'll still have to do a bit of the digging yourself. With that being said, a simple internet search will always come up with a variety of options for you to choose from whether you're looking for programs to help you design your next promotional banner like Canva, or even looking for voice over software like Otter or transcript software like Rev; it's all out there! With a little bit of creativity and a whole lot of drive, you'll find just the right resources to get you from 'point A' to 'point A-mazing.'

Thirdly and finally, you will be unlocking your access to the world. You will be able to target and reach potential customers that you wouldn't have been able to before. Certain social media platforms will even auto translate your promotional posts to the regional language of the area you're promoting in. Is the translation perfect; no, but does it get your foot in the door with potential customers at a fraction of the cost; yes! Remember this: Technology is here to help us - embrace it. I'm not sure why many people resist it. Embrace and grow!

Historically, these 3 unfair advantages over the competition were reserved for the rich. If you didn't have the money to reach enough people in your target market in a timely manner, you would be outdone by the competition who had the financial resources to do so. The internet, in essence, has leveled the playing field in that sense. Now it's all about creativity, public perception and product quality. This historical imbalance is what drove the sentiment that the rich got richer while the poor got poorer, because with enough money, you can make even more of it; wealth begets wealth, so to speak.

With the advent of the internet, now everybody can get in on the action and access DRS abilities. I want to drive a bit of FOMO into your hearts for a minute; that is Fear of Missing Out. The longer you delay in getting to grips with this concept, the longer you will spend missing out on potential income streams. There has never been a better time to start catapulting your business into the spotlight than right now. Everyone is online, especially in a pandemic and post-pandemic world. With more and more people turning to the internet as a means to conduct their jobs remotely and work from home or elsewhere, there has been an upsurge in the amount of internet users. Even mom and dad who ask you for help setting up their new smartphones have gotten to grips with the workings of the web.

So, what does that mean for you?

Simply put, you now have an enormous pool to work from. There was a time when reaching some of your target audience may have been a little difficult via the internet. An ageing population with far less technological knowledge than their younger counterparts meant that for the most part, you still had to reach them with some form of traditional marketing strategy. Now, however, most of this population has embraced the internet as a means for them to communicate with their loved ones, handle their grocery shopping from a safe distance and even fill out prescriptions.

It's a smorgasbord of new faces in potential target audiences that you can tap into right this moment to drive your sales and increase your revenue. All you have to do is seek out the opportunities, keep your finger on the pulse of what is going on in the lives of the target audience, and then activate your DRS in order to maximize on this rise in online revenue.

Gone are the days when the rich had a head start on you in terms of reach. Those days are far behind our generation. Now, everyone is on the same starting lineup. The lines between rich and poor are being blurred, and the possibilities to make something from next to nothing are abounding. It takes laser-like focus and an iron will to get there, though. At the end of the day, what you need to maintain as you unleash your DRS is consistency. I'm sure you've heard the saying, 'consistency is key', before. It's part of why we explored branding in such depth. How you reach your potential customers, and the speed in which you do so, also has to be consistent throughout. Think about it from a customer perspective. Let's say your customer, or potential customer, is used to receiving updates on products from you once a week amongst all of your other data dissemination. Let's take it one step further and hypothesize that they are used to receiving this update from you via Facebook; if you begin to lose the consistency of the day of the week that you post, and the type of information that you post on that specific day, you would be eroding your reach. Believe me when I say, although it's easy to build your reach nowadays, it's equally easy to decimate it. Your customers, both those you are trying to retain and those you are trying to win over, look to you for consistency and relevance. If you are not actively reaching out to them on a consistent basis, you lose your relevance.

Here's what happens. Based on your customers' activity with your page, most social media platforms like Facebook and Instagram add their interest in you into the algorithm; meaning thanks to you, they are going to start seeing more posts related to what you are promoting, offering or posting.

That's great for you; if you're consistent. If you aren't consistent, sooner or later, their newsfeed is going to be filled with similar vendors or service providers and your lack of consistency will most likely end up with you not appearing as much on their feed, or worse, them unfollowing you in favor of a similar, more consistent brand.

So, yes, DRS can be very powerful, but only if you are consistent. If not, you're just helping the next similar brand to take your place with your target audience.

I want to speak about data and speed for a second, because I see this a lot with small time businesses that are trying to grow. I understand that you want to keep inside information private, but your price shouldn't fall into that category. If you feel like you are overpriced and you would like a customer to request a quote in order for you to convince them of your quality, you've already lost the battle. Transparency is the best way to ensure that you are accessing your target markets with speed. People want to know who you are, what you offer and how much it's going to cost them, and they want to know it now. They don't have the time to wait on a quotation or an estimate; at the end of the day there are hundreds of other businesses fighting for their attention who are all being as transparent as possible in order to win sales. I can't tell you how many websites I come across that have no semblance of information regarding the business let alone the product and the price. You don't know what to make of it. Clearly you can see what the brand is trying to represent, but as for what it stands for and what its offerings are, they may as well not have a website at all; if anything, it ruins your credibility. Even a free service is better than a service with no price, as long as you mentioned it.

Think about this before you want to set up avenues to grow your reach; do you have what it takes to drive your own sales? Are you committed to be consistent? Are you conveying it in a transparent manner that allows for a speedy understanding of who you are and what you offer?

If you can't answer any of these questions without a shadow of a doubt, then the chances are that you are on the wrong track. Stop, regroup, read over the first three chapters again and then strategize your way forward. If you're still feeling stumped, don't worry; Chapter 6 is going to help you identify your marketing objectives in a way that won't have you feeling pressured and overwhelmed.

Before we get there, let's just recap this section very briefly, because it is incredibly important. DRS refers to Data, Reach, and Speed. If you can utilize the internet right now, you are going to be cutting back traditional costs that you may have had to endure in order to reach your target market. The internet is going to allow you to reach people that you may have not had the opportunity to reach before and it's going to allow you to do it faster than you can imagine. Collate your data regarding your target audience, and similarly get your data in order that you wish to disseminate in order to maintain an air of transparency. The faster your target audience can get to know you, your offering, and your price, the better off you will be for it. Keep it consistent, and you'll be on your way to a winner.

If you feel like you've been doing everything according to these simple rules, yet you still feel as though you are missing the mark, you may be experiencing failure to launch. Basically, what you're putting in is not what you're getting out. This can be a sad and painful reality for many businesses and managers alike, but there is usually a trail that you can follow in order to determine where you're going wrong. Let's look at this briefly before getting on to your marketing objectives.

CHAPTER 4: RECAP
Exercise That Mental Muscle

1. What is DRS in terms of marketing?

   _____

   _____

2. Can you achieve success online with no marketing budget?

   _____

   _____

3. How has DRS leveled the playing field?

   _____

   _____

4. What is the major cost that you will have to contend with?

   _____

   _____

5. What are the 3 'unfair' advantages that DRS will give you?

   _____

   _____

6. How can you maintain consistency online?

   _____

   _____

7. What will happen if you are inconsistent?

   _____

   _____

8. What does transparency do for your brand?

   _____

   _____

Give it your best, and head to the end for the answers.

Chapter 5:

Failure to Launch

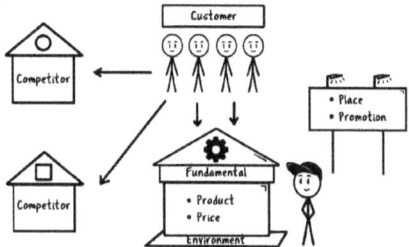

Are you getting the results for what you're putting in?

Do you feel like you have been funneling a significant amount of dollars into what seems like a bottomless pit? If you do, you may be suffering from failure to launch. While a lot of marketers and entrepreneurs will feel as though they are working according to the book, they may still find themselves in a position where their output outweighs their gains - mentally, physically and financially. To put it plainly, expense > income and output > results. It can be an incredibly stressful and tumultuous time for even the most seasoned business professional, but you can find out your efforts to deliberate on where you could possibly be going wrong.

Don't panic! I'm going to show just how you can measure your marketing performance. By the end of this chapter, you'll be able to know how to analyze your own campaign performance and then move on to creating brand new, informed, impactful strategies. Let's jump right in!

First off, review your campaign goals. For example, if you've been actively creating social media campaigns, you should have had clearly defined goals in mind. If you didn't have any to begin with, there is your very first problem. Technically speaking, your campaigns should only ever be geared towards 3 points of interest; growing your sales, increasing your leads, or growing your followers. You need to be able to measure your return on investment. Say, for example, if you are measuring according to a goal of growing your social media followers, you can easily find out how many people were able to find and follow your pages as a result of your campaign. It can be a little trickier when it comes to sales leads, but if you are actively selling products or services online, it is fairly easy to create a lead magnet out of your existing products and services through the use of promotions such as a 14-day trials, or small sample packs to give away. All you need to do is simply set up an 'opt-in' form to offer the lead magnet in exchange for your traffic's name and email on your business product landing page. This is done in order to measure how many leads were generated from the web traffic that was created via the campaign. From there, you can easily measure up how much of that traffic, or leads, turn into a sale and you can measure your sales conversions as a result. You may want to consider A/B testing with two separate landing pages to ensure that your closing approaches are the most effective.

There are 9 prevailing factors which need to be taken into consideration in order for you to successfully measure whether or not what you're putting in is generating enough of what you're getting out. We will delve into performance metrics in further detail later on in, but for now let us mention them quite briefly:

1. Post engagement rate;
2. Website traffic analytics;
3. Customer retention rate;
4. Sales volume and value;
5. Brand awareness;
6. Customer acquisition cost;
7. Lead generation cost;
8. Thought leadership; and,
9. Return on ad spend / investment / effort

You need to be able to measure your return on investment in terms of the aforementioned factors, and you need to do so for every single campaign that you roll out. It's the only way to be absolutely sure that you're not repeating campaign strategies which simply aren't giving you good results.

How do you do it, you might ask?

Well, there are a number of tools at your disposal which you can use right now in order to find out the success or downfall of any campaign.

The first of the lot are your social media analytics. You can most certainly find out how certain posts or campaigns were received; including post engagement, new followers, comments and likes. You might even be able to find out how many people were redirected to your website, so it gets a solid 4 out of 9 for showcasing brand awareness, thought leadership, website traffic generation, and engagement.

Next up are the age-old website analytics. It's important to know how much traffic landed on your landing page, what's the bounce rate, whether your landing page is doing the job you intended them to do. What did the visitors do after landing on your landing page - if you are an ecommerce store, they may sign up for a newsletter, click on to another page; if you have a funnel, they may opt in for your lead magnet. Start referencing back to activities or campaigns that you've rolled out in the past and analyzing them in terms of any potential spikes in traffic around the time that they were rolled out. Did those activities or campaigns cause a spike? If not, what was the reason for it? If it did cause a spike in traffic, how much of that traffic were converted into leads and sales? You could be running a retargeting campaign and you would want to know how much of your audience actually progresses further and take your offer. Work it out as a percentage and then work out what the average profit was on those sales versus what the campaign cost you. If the number is unprofitable, then follow the path that those leads may have taken on your website. Surely, they saw something that interested them; that is why they clicked the link in the first place. However, there may be a flaw in your funnel towards your store or sales channel which deterred them from purchasing. It could be anything - headline, pricing, details on your offer and etc. Where did they click off the page? Was it when they got to the checkout page? If you are selling a physical product, and that is the case, was it possibly due to a high shipping fee? You need to go through your analytics with a fine-toothed comb in order to understand what's stopping them from giving you the details or finishing the checkout process. Remember: Understanding is key here.

Once you have some good understanding on what could be the reasons, take a deeper look at what regions most of your traffic comes from, your least and most frequented pages, the average time spent on said pages and where they click away. This will let you know where your weak and strong points are, so that you can formulate a strategy to address them. It is also quite important that you analyze how your website ranks on search engines, do your keyword research, work on your backlinks, try to find mini successes around your website then try to back track or replicate the process throughout your website.

A lot of people land a windfall due to sheer blind luck. If your sales are increasing that's great, but if you're not sure of the reason why then you could enter a downtrend without knowing how to prevent it. Make sure that you analyze your strengths as much as you do your weaknesses, so that you can build on what you are doing right.

We'll have a look at ROI, or return on investment, and ROAS, or return on ad spend, later on, but for now the takeaway from this chapter should be that in order to figure out why you might not be getting as much out of what you are outlaying, you need to do some deep internal digging. Essentially, based on data, look for signals, clues and insights within your business.

While we're on the subject, head on over to the next chapter to find out if you have some of the core problems which I have seen amongst businesses, and how you can enhance your objectives to combat them.

CHAPTER 5: RECAP
Exercise That Mental Muscle

1. Why are campaign goals important?

   _____

   _____

2. What is A/B testing?

   _____

   _____

3. How will A/B testing help you campaign efforts?

   _____

   _____

4. What are the 9 prevailing factors to take into consideration when you are finding your campaigns?

   _____

   _____

5. What are social media analytics good for?

   _____

   _____

6. What are web analytics good for?

   _____

   _____

7. What should you be looking out for on your web analytics?

_____

_____

Give it your best, and head to the end for the answers.

Chapter 6:

99 Problems and Marketing Shouldn't be One

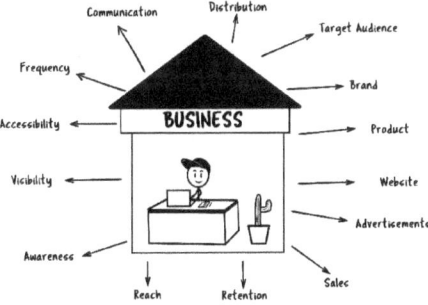

⑤ 14 COMMON PROBLEMS OF BUSINESS

What are your primary problems and objectives?

Before we dive into this chapter, let's take it back to basics for a minute. What is your understanding, or definition, of the word 'marketing'? The problem that I find with a lot of people who reach out to me for help is that they don't even have the faintest idea of what marketing actually is. They think they know, but in actual fact, they barely skim the surface. I'll tell you just why they think that they know the ins and outs of marketing; they think that it's a walk in the park. That's the plain and simple truth. Everyone thinks that they can run successful campaigns because they think that it's easy. You've got a phone, a laptop and some understanding of what it takes to sell; or at least you think you do. If you think that posting fancy imagery with a bunch of 'salesy' text is all that it takes, then you're already headed in the wrong direction.

Listen up; knowing how to create a beautiful Facebook or Instagram post does not automatically make you a marketer overnight. There is so much more to it than that. Think of what you know as being the tip of the iceberg. What you need to know in order to make a success of any marketing campaign lies well beneath the surface. Don't worry, because these next few chapters are going to be the scuba gear that you need to head into those deep waters and come up with life changing insight that is going to totally change the game up for you.

So, this may very well be one of your primary problems; thinking you know something about a certain field that you actually know very little about. There is a reason why major corporations spend top dollar on marketing personnel and campaign efforts. We know what we're doing, and we know how to make money; plain and simple. Before we venture into your objectives, let's have a look at some of these fundamental areas of marketing. These core fundamentals are transferable across the board. It doesn't really matter whether you are conducting marketing online or offline, these principles will remain the same throughout. You need to know what information to put out, when to put it out, where to put it, and then very importantly, how to put it out there. Timing is everything, but so is knowing how to communicate with your target audience. I'm not just talking about verbal communication; I'm talking about all the elements which act as non-verbal cues with your target audience; including posts and campaigns.

In this digital age that we find ourselves in, you may have heard the term 'digital marketing' being thrown around quite a lot. While digital marketing may differ from traditional marketing, rest assured that the basic fundamentals will still remain the same. Nevertheless, let's look at the difference between the two. When all is said and done, we are trying to address problem number 1; not knowing what marketing truly is. The difference between the two is simply that digital marketing are the promotional communication efforts which take place online, while traditional marketing are these very same efforts which take place offline. Essentially, the message will be similar but the delivery will be quite different. So, there you have it; the only difference is the platform on which you deliver your promotional communiqué – that is all there is to it.

This brings us to problem number 2; the fact that the term digital marketing may throw you off your game. Yes, marketing is an immensely involved process that takes creativity, metrics and insight, but ultimately the fundamentals have remained the same over the years. Once you address problem 1, you've already solved problem 2. Let me reiterate it: know your fundamentals! Any new techniques, technologies or platforms will only act in a supplementary fashion towards the core fundamentals.

There are billions of entrepreneurs out in the world right now. Just think of the sheer number of campaigns that are being rolled out on a daily basis. The amount of promotional content being published every day is eye watering. If you don't know the core fundamentals, you will not know how to market your product; and if you don't know how to correctly market your product, you are not going to be any different from the tons of entrepreneurs and their innumerate campaigns. Imagine if there were just 10 buyers ever in history, and there were 100 of you selling the same product. If you all had the same campaigns, with little understanding of the marketing process, none of you would stand out from one another. Left with fairly unlimited choices, those 10 people would engage in a process of trial and error; testing out which of the 100 would supply the best product. If they reached 5th seller out of the 100 and felt satisfied enough not to venture any further, they simply wouldn't. If you're hanging out somewhere around 20th, you've lost the battle already. A good marketing strategy will eradicate the proximity effect, whereby the target audience purchases within convenient proximity and ventures out past 20th seller mark. You have to convince the target audience that you are better than the rest, and you have to do it before they find someone else to fit the bill purely out of convenience.

This is why marketing has always been the leading business function of any successful business. If there is one thing that history has taught us it is that one should never underestimate the potential of what a great marketing campaign can do to transform a business, and similarly that you should never underestimate the level of knowledge that you need going in.

Perhaps you've reached a very difficult situation in your business, and you're seeing a huge decline in your sales. The most painful thing that I have witnessed amongst companies that are going into a temporary decline is that they begin shaving off their marketing efforts. It's almost as if they begin to blame the department for the lack of sales. More often than not, this is not the case at all. You should look to external factors that are going on in the world; the advent of new competition, the economic climate, financial conditions of your target audience that may be a result of some localized event in the chain of normalcy. Whatever it may be, I can almost guarantee you that it is an external pressure being placed on your business, and not a marketing issue. Just deploy some logic for a second, if your marketing efforts have always delivered on the sales targets, but have recently gone into decline, find out the external economic environments as well as the internal work environments before making a call. Sometimes all it takes to rectify the problem is a little reshuffling and a new strategy to address the external or internal pressures.

Without your marketing department in place, there is no way of you reaching out to new customers in order to generate more sales. During a downtrend, a reallocation of resources should be pushed towards marketing in order to migrate back to a survival stance once more. Without marketing there will be no sales; without sales, there will be no income, and without income, your business will inevitably close down.

We've looked at the basics of marketing; the essentials such as the where, when, how, and so on, but I haven't deliberated on the **core** fundamentals. Now that you know the importance of the basics and the importance of your marketing efforts, we can comfortably move on to the 7 core fundamentals of marketing, i.e.:

1. Product;
2. Price;
3. Place;
4. Promotion;
5. Customer;
6. Competitor; and,
7. Environment.

Fundamental	Assumptions / Questions
1. **Product**	What is your product? What does it do? What problems does it solve? Does this product have a constant demand for it?

2.	Price	How much are you selling your product for and is it a justifiable amount? What is your estimated profit per item?
3.	Place	Where are you selling your product online? Where are you selling your product offline? Is it accessible to your target audience?
4.	Promotion	How do you intend to promote your product online? How do you intend to promote your product offline? What is the incentive? Does your promotion create an urge to buy or spark an interest? Is it a promotional-only deal?
5.	Customer	Who is your ideal customer? What does he/she like? What brands interest them? How is your brand similar or dissimilar to these? Where do they hangout? How do they communicate with their friends? What kind of questions or self-conversations would they have in their mind when determining what to buy?
6.	Competitor	Who is your closest competitor? What is their price point in comparison to your own? What are their 7 fundamentals?
7.	Environment	Will your product fair in any environment? Are there certain economic or environmental changes which could render your product redundant? Is your product pandemic proof?

These fundamentals will garner different outcomes for almost each and every business, not only because your product itself may be unique from even the most similar competitor, but also because your way of viewing the fundamentals will differ from other marketers in your industry. It's incredibly important to take note of how your fundamentals relate to your business activities, your target audience and the environment in order for you to strategize campaigns efficiently. If you didn't, you would have denture adverts in the bathroom stalls of bowling alleys that are frequented by kids, and the latest earphones being advertised at your local retirement center. Know your target audience; know who they are, where they hangout, and what their interests are.

Have a bit of fun with it, try listing it out in comparison to your closest competitor and ask yourself some simple questions, such as:

"Is my product better?" If so, *"What makes it better?"* You could also try: *"Is my price higher?"* If so, *"Why is it higher?"* or *"Is my price justifiable?"*:

Fundamental	Assumptions / Questions		
	You	Closest Competitor	Comments/ Findings
1. Product			
2. Price			
3. Place			
4. Promotion			
5. Customer			
6. Competitor			
7. Environment			

This is an example of a simple cheat sheet that I use to find out a product's viability in the market. It will give you a clear perspective on what you can leverage against your competition. Think of it as a peek into your customer's perspective; this is how they analyze you in correlation to your direct competition before they decide whether or not to buy your product or utilize your services, and most of the time they do it without consciously being aware of it. Remember this: I'm sure you heard someone say this before "ignore the competition", you need to listen closely to what exactly they mean. They don't mean to ignore the competition totally; they are asking you to focus on what you do best. Get it?

Your target market is constantly analyzing you in comparison to similar products. None of us want to feel as though we've wasted money. Money is hard to come by, especially during these unprecedented times. Now more than ever, your customers need to feel like they are getting something of value and willing to part with their hard-earned cash to buy from you. You simply have to position yourself as the "better" product; there is no other way to win them over. In my view there is no such thing as 'The Best' product; there are only those that are relatively better than the competition, and marketing has a lot to do with the way your customers perceive you as being the better product. "Better" is the keyword. Think about your own consideration experiences - given a fixed budget, people generally would compare and would go for value and security. Especially if it is your first time buying a certain product - say a Black Sesame Seed Powder - you would look at the price and the packaging. You would compare products and probably pick the one that gives you more value – either that or the one that's won some awards or that has huge claims compared to another product which is similarly priced. As we said before, branding plays a huge role and first impression is important in these situations.

Now, we've covered the core fundamentals of marketing. In order to launch a campaign, we need to be clear from the beginning in terms of what we want to achieve. Sometimes businesses launch a campaign to rectify a problem, other times they launch a campaign to capitalize on an opportunity to drive more results. But what they have in common is, they all start from all these common marketing areas below:

- Target audience;

- Brand;
- Product;
- Platforms;
- Website;
- Advertisements;
- Sales;
- Retention;
- Reach;
- Awareness;
- Visibility;
- Accessibility;
- Frequency;
- Conversion; and,
- Distribution.

Without knowing which area to work on, you will not be able to set clear objectives for your campaign. Without clear objectives, your strategy to achieve your goal will not be clear. You may end up creating more problems for your business than it already has. In fact, this is where most beginners got it wrong - most beginners want to address multiple areas in one campaign. If you successfully achieve the one objective you set, your campaign is a success already. If you can hit two objectives with one campaign, you have an amazing campaign going on. The idea you need to grasp here is focus and do the one thing right. Now, make sure you go through the detail version of each of these areas and find out which area you should focus on. Start by asking these 2 questions in each header:

1. Do you think you have a problem in this area (refer to list above)?
2. Do you see an opportunity to do better in this area (refer to list above)?

Target audience

Do you know your target audience as thoroughly as you need to? We've already briefly looked at how you would need to know certain behaviors such as where they hang out and how they communicate, but it goes a little deeper than that. While there has been a shift away from demographic usage in recent times, there are still certain predetermined elements which will affect how they interact with your product. Elements such a geographic location, cultural and religious practices, age group, and even fiscal standing will impact the buying behavior of your target audience. These factors will help you to define your target audience further and hone in on avenues to communicate with them.

Brand

Is your brand well established? How does your brand promise align with your actual product? You will need to have done an extensive amount of work in this area and this is why we focused quite heavily on branding earlier on Chapter 2. Do refer back if you need to.

Product

Does your product actually fill a need or have you just created something out of personal preference? It is quite a common mistake and an expensive experience that many entrepreneurs make; they love an item so much that they believe surely the rest of the world will too, without actually finding out whether there is a need for the product before investing time and energy into sourcing or producing it. This was a big lesson for me personally in the early days and I learnt it the hard way. There is a great saying from a very popular figure - Tony Robbins - "Model success from those that have already succeeded." There's a huge reason for that, those that have succeeded have proven that whatever the methods or processes they are currently using is working. They have probably invested so heavily in R&D to get there. So, remember this, model success and improvise is the key.

Platforms

You need to be using the right platforms to engage with your target audience. Remember the scenario of having the latest earphones being advertised around a local retirement center. Sure, there is nothing to say that the aged will not buy your product, but your target audience may very well be a much younger demographic. You should, therefore, be engaging them on platforms that they enjoy and use in their daily lives, and in geo-locations where they are predominantly found. Think about what platforms your target audience are hanging out and where exactly are they having their conversations. It could be in a specific Facebook group, Reddit, forums, or an Influencer depending on your niche. I find the best way to do this is imagine yourself having that problem and how would you try to find your answers and solve the problem.

Website

Long the days have gone when having a domain and site is advantageous. Every tom dick and harry has a website now. In fact, they own multiple websites sometimes. It is important to know what type of websites are suitable for your business. It's the reason for the rise of website software like WordPress and Elementor and many popular website platforms like Wix.com, Shopify and Clickfunnels. You've got to know what's good for you! After years of trial and error, I wholeheartedly endorsed both Shopify and Clickfunnels. Both of these platforms are built for the convenience of today's startup entrepreneurs. In short, from my experience, Shopify is more suitable for an E-commerce store where you have many things to sell because it's built for that; Clickfunnels is great for selling one product or one subject focus business and even more effective if you want to sell more of the same thing or upselling supporting product related to your niche. The best news is one needs no programming skills to create their own website on either Shopify or Clickfunnels. One of most incredible things is you can literally create a website yourself within a day if you are starting out and within hours if you have been using it for a while. And, you can edit it easily with a few drag and drop features. I personally created many profit-making sites on both Shopify and Clickfunnels for big clients and myself. So, do check it out and feel free to DM me @tseliang.z if you are interested to build a Shopify site or a Clickfunnels.

Advertisements

Advertisements have never been a bigger topic than anything before, not today. With the rise of the internet, digital advertising has been the major contributor to the creation of millions and millions of individual millionaires. Even after the internet has been here for so long, I can't tell you how many millions of dollars are wasted each year on pointless advertisements. This is only outweighed by the number of entrepreneurs or businesses who are not advertising enough. Advertisements are a direct way to get your product in front of the right target audience. This is not an area to try to cut the budget or cut corners. Invest more in quality or the little you spend will be being poured down the drain and only work towards solidifying your belief that advertisements are only reserved for large scale corporations. Learning new ways of advertising is the only way to stay relevant and to stay ahead in business today. Remember this: The cost of advertising is ever rising but the cost of reaching the target audience you want has never been more affordable today. Not to mention the ability to reach specific audiences was never possible before, not today.

Sales

Many businesses and entrepreneurs simply aren't generating the volume of sales that they need in order to make a success of their ideas. Do not fret! It is a very common situation. Not many businesses are profitable or consistent. Of course there are many factors affecting a business performance from branding to product, traffic to goal setting. It's incredibly important to have clearly defined, realistic sales goals and targets. These targets will inform your performance, and will help guide you as to what you should be doing to optimize your ad spends for sales.

Retention

There are so many brands out there that are what I call 'one hit wonders.' They do an great job at reeling in new clients but they have no strategy in place for how to retain these clients. Client, or customer, retention is the number 1 way to ensure that you have a consistent influx of sales each and every month. It's part of the reason that we pay particular attention towards driving brand loyalty.

Reach

We've already spoken about the immense potential that the internet has for you to reach your customers. You need to leverage as many avenues as possible to grow your reach. Having a narrowed focus is the equivalent to walking around with blinders on; you're not going to maximize on your full reach potential. Remember this: Every reach reinforces your brand awareness and brand presence. It is all these outreach that gives you the upper hand when it comes to deciding the winner.

Awareness

Sometimes, it's not that your product is substandard or undesirable, it's just that there is very little awareness of it. Awareness is a school of thought around top of mind. It has a lot to do with your brand visibility, accessibility and frequency. This is a huge subject on its own and it has a fascinating psychological science work behind it. A true marketer is one who knows and understands the concept of "The Art of Awareness." We elaborate further with visibility, accessibility and frequency.

Visibility

How visible is your brand or product to your target audience? Visibility doesn't just refer to having some sort of physical visibility such as an office, it refers to visibility on a broader spectrum around your target audience and beyond. Essentially - How often are you being seen across the channels physically, out of home and virtually? What can you do to increase your visibility to your audience? In execution, the key question is asking how many channels is your brand present in? Do you have a presence on Facebook? Instagram? Out of home? YouTube? Google? TV? Radio? Newspaper? Magazine? Brand Partners?

Accessibility

Whether you're selling online, in traditional brick and mortar stores, or both, you need to be accessible. Early on during the Amazon rally, many businesses missed out on a potential windfall in certain regions, as shipping to those regions was incredibly expensive and fell on the buyer instead of the seller. While you cannot commit to absorbing all of the costs for your target audience, running the numbers to find out whether or not there is market viability in far reaching regions can gain you astronomic sales. Make sure that your product is accessible. If your product is only accessible to a target pool of 1000 people, and you're expecting millions of dollars in revenue, you're dreaming. Remember this: just by being accessible, you have greatly increased your visibility and in turn raise your brand awareness in general.

Frequency

Remember that we spoke about consistency. Frequency is consistency's cousin. You need to be engaging your target audience on a frequent basis across channels. The goal is to remain relevant even if you are not promoting anything in particular. You need to appear as though you are in constant contact with your customers. Frequency builds visibility and over time this gives off a strong feeling of reliability and security which can be a very strong advantage for your brand. That's what some of the biggest daily brands available today excel in such as Maggi and Nestle. You see them everywhere; you can access them almost anywhere and you hear about them everywhere. Power of awareness and excellence in execution.

Conversion

This is quite possibly the biggest pitfall of any business. Entrepreneurs may have a sizable number of leads but then they just don't know what to do with those leads! Following up on each and every single lead can be a mammoth task for a business of any scale. This is why it is important to have the right method to ease up mammoth tasks, utilizing the latest technology and tools available, have a set of procedures about what responses to use and when to schedule follow-up can save time, effort and cost while maximizing conversion.

Distribution.

Distribution, much like accessibility, can be problematic for some businesses. Depending on the nature of the product, the size, and whether or not it contravenes certain by-laws in varying regions can become a bit of an issue. It is important that you deliberate on a distribution strategy, along with several options for distributors and channels so that you're never left hanging in the lurch.

If you've noticed a problem or an opportunity in any one of these areas, there is a method for you to step back and address it. I call this objective setting. Your objective should answer the following questions:

- What do you need to do?
- What are you trying to achieve / rectify / improve?
- What business problem are you facing currently?
- Why are you having this problem?

Ultimately answering these questions can give you greater insight into the root cause of the problem or an idea so that you can gain clarity and take action. In essence, from here you a clear campaign objective to help you rectify a business problem, or take action on an idea.

Action:	Objective Setting
Why do you want to run a campaign?	
Identify what problem or idea you have right now.	
Why and how did this idea/problem come about? What is the insight?	
• Why?	
• How?	
• Insight 1.	
• Insight 2.	
What do you need/want to do about it? • Write down your main objective (Up to 3)	

When all is said and done, I need you to realize that all ideas are good ideas; it just boils down to whether you have the resources, support and the timing. All problems on the other hand, are bad and you need to solve them as quickly and efficiently as possible. The sooner you do this, the better your revenue will be and the lower your costs will be.

Once you have clear objectives in mind that speak to a particular idea or a particular problem, you can now proceed to take further steps into planning and strategizing in terms of how you want to achieve it. Now, it's not just enough to rectify these problems without knowing what you aspire to get out of it. You also need to be painfully clear about what you hope to achieve in terms of your business and marketing goals - numerically - can be metrics or financial goal. We all have a number as they say, what is yours?

CHAPTER 6: RECAP
Exercise That Mental Muscle

1. Why do people fail at marketing campaigns?

   _____

   _____

2. Are the core fundamentals of marketing the same for online and offline efforts?

   _____

   _____

3. What is the key difference between traditional marketing and digital marketing?

   _____

   _____

4. What is proximity convenience?

   _____

   _____

5. How do you eliminate the proximity convenience problem?

   _____

   _____

6. What is the mistake that many businesses make when they go into a temporary decline?

7. What are the more likely reasons for a temporary decline?

8. What are the 7 core fundamentals of marketing?

9. Why will the deliberation of fundamentals vary across competitors?

10. What are the 14 more common problems of in terms of marketing objectives?

11. Are all ideas good?

12. Are all problems bad?

Give it your best, and head to the end for the answers.

Chapter 7:

Know your Goals

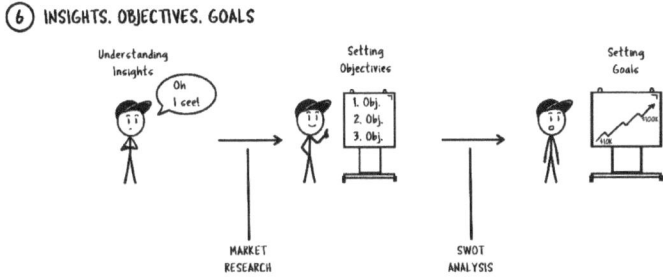

What's your number?

Even when your marketing campaigns are top quality, they might still fall short if you don't have a figure in mind. It's great to say, "I want to grow my sales", but by how much? If you don't have a financial goal in place, you're shooting in the dark. Here's the thing; as an entrepreneur that might be just breaking into your industry, your early goals may involve growing your following, generating more views, and generally increasing your brand presence.

However, these actions are all ultimately geared towards strengthening your chances of hitting your financial goal. When it comes down to it, sometimes it's not about the way in which you are going about your marketing, but the way in which you are planning your targets. Sales targets are vital to a winning campaign; without them, how would you know what you're trying to achieve? Don't be shy about it; leave the modesty behind. In order to achieve the financial success that you desire, you have to be aggressive in your strategies; realistic, but aggressive.

It's always best to start off with a revenue goal. Set this goal with a 12-month deadline, and then break it up into months. If you have a revenue goal of $1,000,000, and you're trying to promote a product that costs $100; you know that you would need to sell 10,000 units to reach that target. Break it down even further into monthly targets; you would need an approximate 835 sales per month in order to reach $1,000,000 in revenue.

Based on your current sales conversion metrics, you would be able to decipher precisely how many leads you would need to go via your site each month based on your conversion rate, or percentage. Numbers don't lie. I truly love that statement. When you get down to the simple mathematics of the system, you'll be able to set clear goals and adjust them based on your metrics, as well as on whether your production capacity can handle fulfilling it.

Be specific and be aggressive! If you're still feeling a little blurred on the subject, try following some of the steps below in order to set clear, realistic but aggressive marketing goals. It can feel like a lot to grasp, but I'm going to break it down for you in a way that is relatively simple to put into use.

Financial Target (12 months)	$1,000,000
Product Price per Item	$100

Total Number of Units needed to reach the 12 Month Target	10,000
Total Number of Units needed to reach the Monthly Target	835

Now let's have a look at the amount of leads needed, and the potential cost in generating those leads.

Assumed closing rate 25%

835 / 0.25 = 3,340 leads needed per month

Assumed advertising cost per lead $9

3,340 x $9 = $30,060 ad cost per month

Revenue per month is 835 x $100 = $83,500

Projected profit is $83,500 - $30,600 = $53,440

At this point you need to find out whether your advertising is capable of pulling this through for you. If you're only getting 1,000 hits a month, you're not anywhere near where your targets are. If you're lucky enough to have a lead conversion rate of 3% on your website, you would need a mind numbing 1,093,333 visitors to your website every single month over the next 12 months in order to reach your $1,000,000 revenue mark.

I think you're starting to get the picture as to why it's important to set your number and then to work out a strategy. The strategizing process will inform you as to how viable your targets really are, and then you can adjust from there. Based on the fact that you can grow your web traffic from upwards of 10% per year, work out what you're reaching right now, and where you could be in the next 12 months. Does it align with your financial goal? Is the goal too aggressive? Is the goal realistic? Once you can answer those questions as honestly as possible and have a healthy profit margin in mind, you will be able to set a good number for your target.

You might still be struggling to set clearly defined goals, and there is a simple acronym that you can use. You may have even heard of it before. The acronym is SMART.

Not only should you be working on financial goals from a number's perspective, you should also be measuring them in terms of how SMART they are. SMART is a goal setting acronym for specific, measurable, attainable, relevant and time-bound. There is a reason why specificity is first up on the list, and this is because if you're not being specific with your goals, you won't have specific methods of reaching them. How do you begin your journey when you're uncertain of the destination? Well, you don't; and if you do, you'll probably get lost along the way.

As an entrepreneur, marketer or business owner, your goals should always be centered around increasing sales revenue via creating brand awareness and increasing target market value through the deployment of high-quality products. Furthermore, there should be a considerable amount of effort geared towards growing thought leadership. Let's have a look at some of the goals you could be setting and how to make them SMART.

In terms of increasing sales, you need to make sure that what you are trying to achieve is possible within the realm of your capacity, and also within the realm of your online presence as well as traffic. We've already discussed how sometimes the goal you have in mind may seem attainable, until you actually work on the calculations for the number leads that you would need in order to achieve it. Depending on the length of your sales cycle and your business model, you need to make sure that your goals are measurable. Performance metrics are the most important factor in a smart goal when it comes to sales goals. If you're struggling to figure this out, head back to the example in this chapter to give you some guidance. Remember, if you don't have a sales history, in the case of fairly new businesses, then work with what you have according to the steps in this chapter and make adjustments as more data comes in.

When it comes to generating leads, it might be a little easier to find out how effective your strategies are. Once you have a sales goal in mind, it's easy to work out how many leads you need to in order to reach that sales target. I need you to bear in mind that not all leads are ready to make a purchase. Especially if you are starting out, they have shown interest in your offer, but I can promise you that most of your leads never heard of your brand before, chances are they are not likely to buy from you immediately. It is absolutely normal. Think about a brand you came across for the first time, what are your chances of making an immediate purchase? Rarely right? Unless they are offering a very good deal and everything is exactly you want it. This happens once in a blue moon. As an entrepreneur, you need to nurture your customers, build up your relationship, increase your credibility, constantly give value to your customers. There are several stages that a general lead has to go through before they can become a sales qualified lead. I generally categorize all leads into 4 stages - awareness, consideration, purchase, and retention. Most leads that you acquired through your website or funnel are generally in the awareness or consideration stage. The best practice is to assume all leads are in the awareness stage.

Once you understand the concept, different communication strategies are required to communicate with customers at different stages so that the message stays relevant and your chances of moving them through the stages is higher and eventually converting them into paying customers. You will also want to work out how many of them you can retain. This is subject to your business model. Retention generally means re-purchase of the same products. If you are selling a one-off product, this may not apply to you but your post-sale services may be applicable. Your retention figure should be worked out on a ratio. If you know that you've retained 80% of your customers, then you've failed to retain 20% of your customers. Make sure that you have clear goals as to how much retention you would like to see in the financial year ahead, as well as your strategy to sustain the retention rate you want. Find out all possible causes for any negative retention development, both external and internal factors, and address them. Always, make the goal SMART. In this case the duration of your timeline would be 12 months. To make the goal specific and measurable, you could opt to set it as follows: "We want to ensure our customer retention rate is at least 70% over the next 12 months." Since you have your figures on your current customers, and a strategy for retention, it will be easy to measure whether or not you've attained the goal at the end of the cycle.

The best way for you to retain customers is to increase customer satisfaction. Would you spend money on a product that is being sold by an unreliable, grouchy or unfriendly person or brand? I mean, no matter how good the product is, if the purchasing experience and engagement with the brand thereafter is deplorable, are you really going to want to head back there? A big part of us spending our hard-earned cash is feeling as though the business that we're engaging with appreciates us and is worthy of our money. If you aren't focusing on customer service, you're effectively walking away from some really low hanging fruit that is ready for picking. The internet is once again here to save the day. If you don't have the budget to conduct lengthy surveys at the moment, you could always consider setting a poll up on your social media pages. Facebook has an array of tools to help you conduct surveys with your customers so that you can get down to the bottom of what might be troubling them and what you're doing right, so that you can build on that. This is also a great way to measure how many people came across the survey, how many people actually clicked on it, and how many people successfully completed it.

KNOW YOUR GOALS

The final two overarching goals that you may want to consider are launching new products and up-selling. I want to start off with up-selling because it is such an effective way to make more money without having to bring in an additional customer. Your customers that are satisfied and willing to continue purchasing your products or services may be ready for up-selling. Up-selling involves doubling up on a current customer's sale, either by offering them an add-on to the current product or service they are purchasing, or more of the very same; depending on the nature of what you're selling. Right now, in this digital age, up-selling is responsible for anywhere between 15%-30% of any given e-commerce store's sales. That's up to one third of your overall sales! Can you imagine the sheer volume of sales revenue increment that you could achieve by up-selling? I definitely recommend that you take the SMART goal approach and plan some up-selling target figures for the year ahead.

Now, this links quite closely to launching a new product. You can also cross-sell to existing customers. Effectively, you're creating a space for them to think, "Well, I liked the first product that I bought from them, I'm sure I'll like this new one just as much." When you launch new products or services, always be sure to add your existing customers into the early stages of your target. They can actually be a great resource for you in terms of 'word of mouth' marketing and these cross-sales can account for about 10% of your overall revenue.

Work on your 'number' across the board. Figure out the sales revenue you want to generate per product or service, your customer retention number and their respective revenue. Ideally, you want to have numbers for it all.

Once you have clear financial goals in mind, everything else will be created to fall in line with them; from your monthly budget to your marketing campaigns.

CHAPTER 7: RECAP
Exercise That Mental Muscle

1. Why are sales targets vital to campaign success?
   _____
   _____

2. How should you section your goals – daily, monthly, annually, or other?
   _____
   _____

3. What is an opportunity?
   _____
   _____

4. What is a general lead?
   _____
   _____

5. What is a marketing qualified lead?
   _____
   _____

6. What are sales qualified leads?
   _____
   _____

7. What is a healthy profit margin?

8. What is the average growth you can achieve for your website, year-on-year?

9. What are SMART goals?

10. What is retention?

11. What is the best way to increase customer retention?

12. Where can you conduct affordable surveys?

13. What is up-selling?

14. How much of an ecommerce store's sales are generated by up-selling?

_____

_____

15. What is cross-selling?

_____

_____

16. How much do cross sales account for in total revenue?

_____

_____

Give it your best, and head to the end for the answers.

Chapter 8:
Strategize Like A Strategist

Are you being specific enough with your SWOT?

Once you've reached this point, you might feel as though your goals are still a bit too vague; after all, we haven't addressed how these goals align with your business model. When you started up your business, or began the research phase, you will most likely have conducted a form of SWOT analysis. It is imperative that we revisit that analysis now and see if there are any strengths and opportunities that you can further build on in order to have a more detailed goal. You might also want to have a good thought on your business weaknesses and threats. It's going to do you a world of good in terms of analyzing what prevailing factors might be steering you off course, and what opportunities you may have missed to exploit along the way.

Once you have the broader spectrum SWOT in plain sight, I want you to work on a deeper SWOT analysis that focuses specifically on your marketing efforts. More often than not, we are just not utilizing and leveraging all of the resources at our disposal. Take the following table into account when you are trying to work on a SWOT analysis from a marketing perspective:

	QUESTIONS/ ACTIONS	COMMENTS
STRENGTHS	1. List your company's strengths. 2. Compare your marketing initiatives to that of your closest competition. 3. List the resources that you have at your disposal to help you reach your current objectives.	
WEAKNESSES	1. List your company's weaknesses. 2. Are there areas where your marketing proves less effective than that of your closest competition? 3. List the resources that you wish you had at your disposal to help you reach your current objectives.	

OPPORTUNITIES	1. List your company's opportunities. 2. What is the competition not addressing via their content? 3. What trends are relevant enough to your industry that you should be capitalizing on?	
THREATS	1. List your company's threats. 2. What is the competition currently doing in terms of marketing that you are not, and why? 3. What, if any, are the prevailing conditions that are hindering you from achieving your objectives?	

All in all, you need to get down to the very root of what you are trying to achieve and what prevailing factors might be hindering you from achieving it. Your goals need to be specific to your niche, your industry and conducting an analysis with a close comparison to your competition can give you fantastic insight at a fraction of the cost and possibly saving you a hefty price in the future.

So, you've got further insight into how you've positioned yourself amongst the competition, and you now want to put some actual strategies in place that will then feed into a tactical plan. Great! Let's get to it.

Having a Strategy in Place

When it comes to strategizing, you need to have clear strategies for all of your goals. These strategies need to have different approaches. Why? To put it simply; your messaging and your promotions are going to be different depending on what you're trying to achieve. You can't just have the same approach to every single strategy, because their outcomes are going to be different, and thus the methods will need to be different too.

Let's take three hypothetical objectives into account here:

1. Increase revenue through digital sales channels;
2. New product launch; and,
3. Increase consumer engagement.

All three of these are objectives to help you grow your brand and your sales, but they are all very different. It's important that you break them down further to get to the root of how to plan tactically for each of them. Think of the accompanying goals that would be paired off with each objective. This will encompass your strategy.

OBJECTIVE	GOAL
Increase revenue through digital sales channels;	Increase total revenue by $1M by Dec 2021
New product launch; and,	Launch Product by July of 2021
Increase consumer engagement.	To have 10M video views by Dec 2021

Do you see how the goal needs that specificity that we've been talking about? You don't want to just increase revenue; you want to increase revenue by a very specific number. In this case, $1,000,000. This is how I want you to strategize your moves in your business; with the specificity of knowing the measure and the timeline of your target. It is at this point that you can move on to tactical planning.

Before we dive straight into how you can move these steps from mere strategies to a tactical plan, we're going to kick the next chapter off with some of the means and mechanics, before we get into the details. Coming up is your tactical planning!

CHAPTER 8: RECAP
Exercise That Mental Muscle

1. What is a SWOT analysis?

   _____

   _____

2. What are marketing strengths?

   _____

   _____

3. What are marketing weaknesses?

   _____

   _____

4. What are marketing threats?

   _____

   _____

5. What are marketing opportunities?

   _____

   _____

6. How can you use this to address your marketing failures?

   _____

   _____

7. Why do you need to have different strategies for each goal?

   _____

   _____

Give it your best, and head to the end for the answers.

Chapter 9:

Time for Campaign Planning

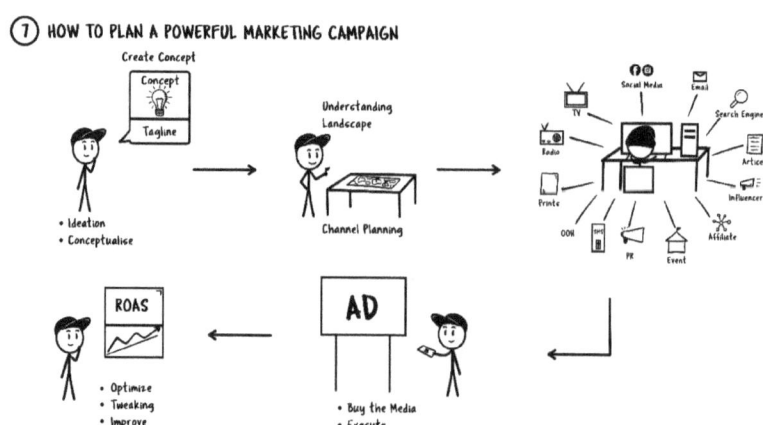

Get a 360 Campaign Marketing Plan Together

We've gone through goal setting quite extensively at this point, now it's time for you to put all of that information into practice and deliberate on your 360 campaign marketing plan. As the saying goes, if you're failing to plan, you're planning to fail. Many entrepreneurs have absolutely brilliant products, but they never seem to pull in the figures that they should be pulling in. This is almost always due to a lack of an effective marketing campaign; I'd even go so far as to say that this failure is 99% due to ineffective campaign concepts, channels and tactics. You can't just roll out a new product, put up a billboard and hope for the best. You gotta understand your target audience, what their life looks like, where they like to hangout online and physically, how do they solve their current problem, why are they having this problem, what channels do they use to find a solution. There's a great deal of benefit from trying to understand your target audience, you will have insight into what they will like, and you will be able to craft a message that speaks to them, and you will have a better idea on where to promote your offer and reach them. Make it a habit to build your target audience profile and try to draw out their lifestyle. It will be invaluable as you plan your marketing campaign.

Campaign Concept & Tagline

Once you understand your core audience, it's time to get creative and think of the overall campaign concept that speaks to the target audience at all levels across the channel. I'm sure you have seen some powerful marketing campaign that captivates you before, here's some notable ones such as:

- Nike: "Just Do It" Campaign
- Apple: "Get a Mac" Campaign
- Volkswagen: "The Last Mile" Campaign
- Marlboro: "The Marlboro Man" Campaign
- Coca-Cola: "Share a Coke" Campaign

You may have noticed that all these powerful campaigns have some very similar elements such as a clear campaign tagline, they are activated on at least 2 or more channels, simple mechanics with one message to speak to the target audience. It is essential to have a clear campaign concept and tagline because it allows your campaign to scale effectively and seamlessly across channels and regions. If your campaign concept can tap into your audience's emotions, give them assurance and convince them you are the logical choice, you would have a very successful campaign.

This is the first step towards building a successful marketing campaign. What makes a successful marketing campaign you may ask? Aside from having the perfect campaign concept and tagline, it greatly depends on the goal metrics you set, as long as you achieve the goal metrics, your campaign is a success. For example: if your campaign goal is to launch a product by Dec 2022 and you launch your product by Nov 2022, it's a success. If your campaign is to achieve 1 million views on your video on Youtube by Dec 2022, and you only have 800k views by Dec 2022, your campaign is not a success then. Hence, why we went through so much on goal setting in the previous chapters because goal setting is really important when it comes to marketing campaign planning.

Understanding The Landscape

Before we dive into marketing campaign planning, I want to spend a little time on explaining the concept of "Understanding The Landscape" and the idea of "Own, Borrowed, Paid". In the olden days when war was happening around the world, the general plays a very important role in coming up with a strategy to win a battle - whether it is to attack or defend. First he will try to understand the landscape of the battlefield and usually he will mark all the key locations such as the high ground, the low ground, the valley, the water line, the hole, and many other things. Once he understands the full landscape, he then strategically devises a battle plan that gives him the highest chance of winning the battle. The general will always plan to play to his strength to neutralize any threats and take advantage of any opportunities and

TIME FOR CAMPAIGN PLANNING

the enemy's weakness. With that, he will strategically plan all resources that he owns, resources that he could borrow and resources that he could pay for and allocate them across the battlefield. Each key location that he decides to allocate resources, he will make sure he has some form of tactic in place to help him win. Example: He may position a scout on a strategic high ground to help him lookout for enemy movements and report to him periodically. He may set up a trap to lure an enemy into the valley. He may cut off the supply of water to the enemy's camp if the negotiation fails. The list goes on. Now, can you see the linkage with marketing campaign planning? It has a close resemblance on how we plan certain marketing tactics within a marketing campaign. Think of the marketplace as the battlefield, think of all the types of marketing channels as the high ground or the valley, and finally think of the tactics you will use to reach your customers as the tactics the general will use on a high ground. Let me put it in a simple format:

- Winning the battle = Successful marketing campaign
- Marking the key location = Picking the right channels
- Tactical win at each key location = Tactical success at each channel

So, with every tactical goal you achieved means you are succeeding at the channel, multiplying success across other channels, you would have a successful marketing campaign. So succeeding at each tactical level is key to your campaign success. Now you get the idea, let's dive into the channels that you could use for your marketing campaign.

Website

Let's start with a website. The dotcom era has been here for a while. The internet landscape has changed dramatically with the advancement of technology. Having a website is no longer an advantage to a business. In fact, if you do not have all the right parts to a website that is expected today, it could be a huge disadvantage to your business and your branding. I will not delve into how a great website should be like or what a great website should have because there are literally thousands of articles or videos talking about that. We shall focus on the importance of the website. With that being said, having a great website can drastically change one's life today. Plus, anyone can easily build a website without any programming skill today. There are platforms like Shopify and Clickfunnels - with an affordable monthly subscription, one can start a website easily. I have personally created many websites myself and the website is still the most important channel compared to any other channels available on the internet. Why? Because it's yours and you own it literally 100%. Anything else you do on Facebook, for example, ultimately it's not yours. Imagine one day, Facebook decided to close down. All your followers are gone. However, everything has it's risk, as long you are aware of the risk you are taking, you should be fine. Aside to that, your website is like your base where every activity should direct the traffic back to your base where you capture the audience details, where you offer your product or service, where the sale happens. Why do that? In time, people will start heading to your website directly when they know what they want instead of wasting time going through all the other channels. With all digital marketing spearheading the ROI for any business, a website is essential for marketing success today. With Google analytics, you can easily find out how many people are visiting your website, specifically which pages, how long they spent, and more. With Pixel and Tag manager, you can easily retarget your audience who visited your website. This is a very powerful tool and is the key difference that differentiates traditional marketing and digital marketing. If you have been hesitating whether you should start your own website, hesitate no more. A website will greatly increase your campaign success because of all the benefits I stated above. Remember this: no matter what you do, always make sure your website is part of the big picture.

Social Media

Social media is a perfect channel for people to connect with each other. No one foresaw a big transformation was coming 20 years ago. But today, almost everyone from a teenager to your grandma now has a social media profile. Partly thanks to Steve Job for inventing the iPhone - the smartphone. It has totally transformed the lifestyle of how people interact with each other today. With like-minded people starting to congregate together online, social media rises with the tide to meet the demands. Hence, over the last 15 years, we have seen so many social media platforms popping up - the likes of Facebook, Instagram, Twitter, Linkedin, Pinterest, TikTok, Clubhouse, the list goes on and they will keep coming. And I do not foresee any slowdown at least for the next 10 years. Hence, as a business today, it is absolutely important to have a social media presence today in order to stay relevant and at the same time being able to reach out to your target audience. With the ability to pixel your audience, social media has allowed many marketers the ability to retarget audiences and be able to craft specific messages and offer to reach the most valuable niche audience. This was a breakthrough itself. No marketing channels were able to do that 20 years ago. Not at this specificity. Hence, it is essential for you as an entrepreneur or business owners to understand the concept of how social media works and pick the right social media platforms that gives you maximum leverage to achieve your marketing campaign goals.

I will not dive specifically into each platform because it will be endless and probably by the time i finish writing this book, my ideas could have been obsolete. Hence, I will be looking at social media as a channel as a whole and talk about evergreen tactics that you could use no matter what social media it is. If you take a step back and look at how all the social media platforms, they have a lot of similarities amongst them. Many popular social media platforms allows people do these few things:

- Post something - texts, images or videos
- Like, Love, Funny, Thumbs Up... the post
- Comment on the post
- Share the post
- They allow hashtags in each post
- They allow tagging of friends in each post
- They also allow tagging of places in each post
- They recently allow people to buy something through a post
- Aside from profiling - anything else is not popular most of the time...

Now that you know social media platforms allow people to do these 'few' things, how hard could it get? In order to go viral, your post content just has to fulfill these 3 criterias - likable, invites a comment, and shareable. Now you may ask what makes it likable, invites a comment and shareable? It's no rocket science honestly, depending on your niche and your brand positioning, so here's another 4 things to remember, your social media post needs to have these elements:

- Attractive
- Relatable
- Relevant
- Value

No matter whether it is a post or an ad on social media, I have seen many successful social media campaigns, they all have a combination of these elements. Luxury brands focus mostly on attractiveness, relatability and relevance. Services focus on a lot of value and relatability. You have to figure out what's best for you based on your value proposition and the brand image you want your customers to think of you. The key to really succeeding on social media is to strive for a unique brand voice.

Email

The good old e-mail. E-mail has come and gone over the years with so many debates and discussions on it's effectiveness. But I can tell you with all my experiences, e-mail will give any business the highest return overtime or lifetime value (LTV) per customer when compared to any other channels. Why? We will come to that shortly. E-mail is the only form of traffic you own and it is also the traffic which you can control freely in terms of timing. With the rise of other forms of marketing channels such as social media, influencer, affiliate - e-mail is easily overshine by the others. It is absolutely understandable because e-mail has been around the longest. This is in fact the best testament to e-mail, it has lasted through the ages and it's usage is without a doubt massive. Think about it - literally everyone has at least one e-mail address. As long as you send to a correct address, the person will receive the e-mail in the inbox. The only question is - will the other person open the email?

I will not go through the debate in terms of skippability and efficiency. But we will talk a little about probability and what makes the other person want to open the email. My teacher once told me that "Nothing is certain in life except death and taxes." So, I thought to myself "Why do anything then since everything is uncertain?" right? So, it has been bothering me the whole day, later I got home and I asked my godfather the same question just to see what he answered. He simply said "Well, nothing is certain for sure, it's what you do about it to increase the chances of certainty." And suddenly, everything starts to make sense to me. No wonder he always said "Preparation is key to everything. As long as you are prepared for the thing that you're gonna do - anything - you will be fine." I finally understand what he has been saying for years. It is the same for getting the other person to open the e-mail, we have to prepare. We have prepare from the headline, the language, the tone and manner, to optimize the time to send the e-mail. Every bit of this preparation increases the probability of the other person opening the e-mail. There's only 3 things that matter for e-mail marketing:

- Headline that speaks to your e-mail audience
- Content that shows great value, relatability and sparks urgency
- Clear call-to-action

The next step is building an email list. A name and an email address will be a good start. Data means information. With information, brands and businesses can make better decisions. This is particularly true since we are in the digital era. You may want to try to profiling your customers and have as much information on your customers as possible once they have opt-in. Knowing whether your customers own a house, their income level, what is their color preference, interest and hobbies can give you great insight and allows you to craft a message that speaks to them, this simple act alone greatly increases your e-mail conversions and reduces your effort and money on advertising. Enjoy the process, make it fun, catchy and more importantly, as long as you make your customers feel that you know them really well, you will do well in e-mail marketing. Always remember this - the more personal the information the better. Start preparing.

Search Engine

Search engines have transformed lives. Library used to be the knowledge centre of the world. It is no longer the case today. Knowledge can be attained at your fingertip with a few taps on your smartphone at a small fraction of cost. With information easily accessible to people, it takes a little bit more effort on keywords research to get a paying customer. When it comes to search engines, it is important to know how it works, how it ranks keywords and how it decides which website comes first, there are thousands of books and videos out there that talk about that, so I will not be talking about this. I will also not be talking about search engine optimization here, but I will cover that in the content channel section in this chapter. I will mainly focus on how search engines can help you to achieve success for your campaign via pay per click method. Depending on your business, some businesses are brand focus while some businesses are service focus. Make sure to find out where you belong. Here's an example:

- Brand focus business are like Nike, Louis Vuitton, and Hublot
- Service focus business are like copywriting, backache treatment, and car detailing

The real deal is understanding what keywords or word phrases your potential prospect would use when searching for solutions on search engines. You may want to do a survey to find out how your prospect searches for answers on search engines depending on where they are in their customer journey phases for brand focus business or problem phases for service focus business. Generally I categorize them into 2 stages:

- Stage 1: Awareness of a need or a problem
- Stage 2: Consideration of options based on brand relevance, brand promise and pricing.

Generally most people who are in stage 1 will go through a form of education to equip themselves with knowledge of their need or problem. People generally search and read up on articles and reviews to educate themselves on what's best for them. So you may want to consider putting search engine optimized (SEO) articles on the subject that they are searching for to tap on that traffic. Once they have enough information on hand, they naturally move into stage 2 where they are in consideration mode. This is where the tricky part happens, it is a little more straightforward for brand focus business because people generally have some form of brand preference. As long as the pricing is acceptable, they will go for the brand they prefer. If there is no brand focus or it is a service focus business, then everything is a 50/50 from here because competition is simply overwhelming. Your prospect will not be able to differentiate who is better. Hence, I mentioned you may need a little effort on keywords research to get a paying customer earlier. You will need to know exactly what keywords and phrases your prospect is searching for in order to win paying customers on search engines. So, it will come down to who appears first in search engines or who speaks to their inner voice better or who appears more on other channels. Think of your own experience, how do you decide which restaurant to go to when you are on holiday in a new city. Preference comes first then reviews and copies that speak to you. For example: You probably wanted italian food only and then you decide which italian restaurant to go to based on which restaurant appears at the top 3 or copies that speaks to you in their reviews. The key here is to understand your prospect languages.

Articles

Article is one of the best educational channels any business can deploy. They are there to serve the very purpose of educating potential prospects on a subject and guide them to the next step. It has proven to nurture warm audience into hot audience. If you are unfamiliar with the 3 temperature audiences "cold, warm and hot" - cold means someone who has never heard of your offer, warm means someone who have seen your offer and may be interested to know more and hot means someone who has great interest in your offer and is ready to make the move very soon. Articles are generally pretty straight forward, it often offers straight up value to readers. In order for your article to do well for your campaign, here's 4 things you have to do properly:

1. Research your topic;
2. Come up with content angles and headlines that speak to the specific audience you are targeting;
3. Address all their concerns and questions they are looking for and;

4. Link it together with your offering.

With a well SEO researched article, it can generate massive organic traffic for your business over time. Just remember to update the article as the time goes by in order to stay relevant. Here's a tip, you could run an ad campaign to bring cold audiences to read your article and retarget those people who read your article but did not go to your website sales page. That way, you would constantly nurture and move people to become hot audiences. Just make sure you have something up your sleeves to sweeten the deal and close them when the audience reach your sales page, or else someone else will.

Influencer

With the rise of social media, like the concept of AirAsia, now everyone can be an influencer. There is no rule in the game of influencer. Literally anyone can be an influencer. Hence, we have seen waves after waves of young influencers coming from social media channels over the years. We have also seen companies using more influencers vs. celebrities for their marketing campaign today. I have worked with hollywood actors, celebrities, talents and influencers and I can tell you the influencers are a mess in almost every way. The only common thing about them is they are all a pain in the a** to deal with. But as time goes by, companies and marketers have become smarter at selection and vetting the influencers. Here's a few tips on how to select an influencer that can help you achieve your campaign success:

- Match his/her content value vs. your brand relevance
- Match his/her follower's profile vs. your offering
- Overall authenticity of the influencer as a whole

If you feel any of the above does not tick, you can forget that influencer because your instinct will save you a lot of money and hassle down the road. Another thing is that I would always take a pinch of salt with the numbers of following and engagement rates because those are manipulatable elements which is why I didn't put that as a tip above. You need to look deeper and closely at the influencer - you gotta communicate with the influencer to find out his/her passion for his/her work and his/her credibility. Just be genuine in your own approach, explain your goals and see how they react to it. You will know it immediately when you find yourself a suitable influencer for your campaign.

Affiliate

Affiliate marketing is the dark horse of the internet. With everyone seeking to make a fortune off the internet, it may feel like there is an infinite amount of wealth hidden in the internet. But if you understand the power of economics, the amount of money the world has is pretty fixed at any given time unless you look at it over a period of time, so with that in mind, there will always be winners and losers. Whoever does better in marketing generally gets more share of the total money, that's it. With that being said, there is only so much marketing resources a small business has, this is where affiliate marketing comes in.

Many small businesses or new businesses do not have the resources to run an extensive marketing campaign, hence most of the time they resort to a more performance-commission based format which is affiliate marketing. It's a great way to increase your revenue without having to invest too heavily in it. In fact, it can be one of the most cost effective yet rewarding tactics out there. The affiliate will be feverishly promoting your product or service for you because the more sales that they make for you, the more money they make in commission. If you have not tried affiliate marketing before, there is more benefit than consequences. There are a few ways to go about it but generally you would have to come up with a 2 things:

- How much commission to give per item sold?
- Commission tiering to encourage more sales? More commission after the affiliate hits a certain threshold (can be in units or value)

Once you have the above, you could either host the affiliate program yourself and recruit the affiliates or you could sign up for an affiliate network such Clickbank or Digistore24 and many other more to list your product or service for affiliates to pick up automatically. The choice is yours. The only difference is that the affiliate network will take a cut from you since they provide you the platform but they give you more exposure and volume.

Another angle I want to cover is that an influencer can be a great affiliate as well, you may pay an influencer for promoting your products or services. Whether their influence pushes a single sale to you or not, that is something you would have to test to find out. However, as long as the matching of your product and influencer is compatible, you should be getting a decent result. Most influencers have a far greater reach than the average affiliate, so they will definitely draw the numbers in for you. Just make sure you negotiate a solid commission term with the influencer before you start any promotion activities, you could save yourself some hard time dealing with their unreasonableness later.

PR

The paparazzi! From the newspaper, magazine, TV channels to online niche portals. The media had the time of their lives before the internet boom. With so many channels available today, the competition landscape has changed tremendously and they no longer had the same bargaining power they used to have. But it does not mean PR is an outdated channel, many media outlets have gone through digitalization over the last 10 years and have many valuable platforms to support the needs of their clients today. If you are planning for a new product launch, PR is still one of the best channels to drive some excitement before the launch. There are a few types of PR activities you could do:

- Press Release
- Media Launch - Interviews and Previews

Press releases are generally low value as it does not have any close engagement with the media. Whereas a media launch is always exciting and yield valuable experiences, with cocktails and finger food, sneak peak moments with the company representative, first touch experience with product before release to market, photo taking opportunities, close encounter with celebrities and more. If you have the budget, go for the bigger experience. The media will do you a great favour and write you a great story. Now, if you are starting out, you do not have a media list, the best way to do it is to go through a PR agency. Most PR agencies keep a list of media outlets, they can help you to pitch your story to both old and new media outlets, write and disseminate press releases and other material you want to give to the media, they will also monitor and alert you if any of their media cover your story. Overall, it's a small fee to pay for exposure and coordination. The key is make sure you get a good PR agency to run your PR activities. There are things you spend and there are things you save, PR is not one of those things you should save on.

TV

Who still watches TV? You probably heard that many times but the fact is that people are watching way more TV than before. Yes, there was a time when TV was overthrown by laptops, PC and mobile. With the likes of Netflix and technology advances, people are connecting so much more devices to consume content on TV. Cable TV stations are going through a series of digitalization, soon we will see a huge come back from them in the form of apps. As a business owner, your role is to understand what TV channels are your audience watching. Your audience could be watching Disney Channel via Youtube on TV or HBO via Astro Go on TV. There are channels where you can place adverts on, focus on those niche channels that suit your product and place your media buys. If your audience is consuming content on Youtube, you just need to start Youtube Ad. This is in fact very easy to get away with. However, if your core audience is consuming content on Fox Sports via Cable TV, then you gotta talk to the TV station. They generally have a rate card that tells you the numbers of TV spots, prices of peak hours and off-peak hours, then you decide how many spots to buy. Buying TV spots on Cable TV channels are not cheap, but they can easily make or break your marketing campaign. This is generally not recommended for startup and small businesses. I would only advise you to go into TV if your business is at least more than 7-figure in revenue for the past 2-3 years, and you have fully explored every other channel possible in this chapter. Otherwise, leave this as your last option. The key is to find out how your audience are consuming content on TV and follow the trail.

Radio

Again, who still listens to the radio? I'm sure you have heard that many times. It depends on who you are targeting. The one thing I learned in the past is that you never write off any ideas no matter what others are saying. And the most important role as a marketer is to always stay objectively focused. You want to imagine living the life of your target audience, be in their shoes and imagine their touchpoints. Then it comes down to asking yourself a few of these key questions:

- Who would be most likely "exposed" to radio?
- At what moments people are likely to be exposed" to the radio?
- How do people tune in to radio today?

These questions will tell you the shift of patterns in your country. It varies across the world. Many people tune in to the radio everyday via their smartphone. Many still listen to the radio when they drive to work or commute to work. Your goal is to find relevance and decide whether you should do anything via radio. If executed with great insight and timing, radio can provide the uplift to give you that cut through you need for a short period of time. Pay attention to who's placing ads on radio to get some ideas. Here's a tip, radio would not be effective if it is the only channel you activated, think of radio as a tide booster and a great support, whatever you do on social media, TV or billboard, radio will greatly reinforce the brand impression and message.

Print

Print used to be the pinnacle of advertising like bows and arrows - the newspapers, magazines, comics, posters, banners, standees, billboards and the rest. With digital platforms taking over the world like a tsunami, print has lost its position to digital print. It was an eventuality. Given the flexibility, sizing, costing and the turnaround time, digital print greatly triumphs over traditional print. However, it does not mean print has lost all of its favour for all situations. Because prints are tangible and expensive to produce, it's value has greatly appreciated in the form of collectibles and exclusivity. If you are hosting a conference or a prestigious event, it does not matter whether it is a physical event or an online event, a beautiful exclusive invitation card speaks a lot more than a digital invitation card. It shows class, respect and command attention more than anything else. Your turnout rate would have a drastic difference compared to if you just send a digital invitation card. This is one of the best ways to utilize print today. Imagine everyone else is saving cost and you are sending a physical invitation card, who do you think they would be more likely to to give their money to? The key is to know what to print and when to use print. Everything has its effects and your role is to decide when to use it to it's maximum effectiveness to help you achieve your campaign goals.

Out-Of-Home (OOH)

Out-of-home (OOH) used to be all printed materials - from billboards, posters, transportation skin takeover, directories, to shopping mall placements and etc. It has transitioned heavily with the availability of LED boards and screens. We will be going a little deeper for OOH in this section. The purpose of OOH advertising remains pretty much the same - drive mass eyeballs, create visibility and enhance brand reinforcement. However, strategic placement has become increasingly important with operators stuffing in more and more advertisers in the same LED screens to maximize their revenues and not yours while charging you based on numbers of eyeballs is ridiculous and unfair to you. To maximize effect, I generally suggest to go for exclusivity placement and full takeover - meaning you are the only advertiser for that particular board at the location. Why? Because it guarantees visibility and reach. What's happening now is that the LED board rotates every 10 or 20 or 30 seconds depending on how many advertisers are in it, by the time it's your turn to show your ad, you have missed out most of the audience already. OOH are very similar to real estate business, the key idea is always location. It doesn't matter the quantity, it's the quality of the location. Imagine you placed a fixed non-rotating billboard at a crossroad where millions of people and vehicles alike pass by in a month vs. a billboard at an awkward corner of a neighbourhood. What do you think the results comparison is gonna look like? The idea is to always place your OOH ad where high traffic of relevant audience with a 5-10% chances of other audiences can see it easily everyday. And all you need is one good location to get the results you want unless you have plenty of budget to splash. There are always a few good locations within a city.

Events

Nothing beats a close encounter. Events are the best way to deliver your brand vision and experience through simulation, demonstration, imagination and realization. With that being said, events are also the easiest way to damage your brand if something doesn't go well. I have personally created many events before from new product launch, brand relaunch, press conference, media previews, exhibits, roadshow, and the biggest was Asia Comic Con. Here's a few tip to creating your own successful event:

- Know your event goals
- Know exactly how you achieve your goals
- Have your checklist, timetables and your rules
- Give clear instruction to your team
- Always have a backup plan if anything fail

These tips are highly condensed statements that I accumulated over the years. It may sound like you know it. That is the moment where you will take a step back and start taking action on these or you will definitely miss the details. Don't say I never warn you. I have learned it the hard way and I would wish someone could have told me back then. With the pandemic as the new norm, people may be shifting to the digital space but events will make a comeback bigger than before after the pandemic. Watch out for it.

SMS

SMS may sound like a channel but do not write this off immediately because it can still deliver incredible results. Depending who you are trying to reach. People constantly have their phones in their hands, and you can pay to have a short SMS promotion sent to their devices. Of course, you will need to have permission to send messages of this nature through to them, but once you have them on a subscription list, you can easily send through promotions, coupons, and even surveys! While e-mail marketing is great and cost effective, the open rate for most promotional e-mails is generally less than 20%, while SMS promotions are opened at a right of 95%. What you need to keep in mind is that, you can't deliver as much information in an SMS as you can in an e-mail, so your copy needs to be on point. Every single word counts; literally. Knowing when to use this mechanic can be the difference between make or break. It's incredibly powerful, but age group dependent, so do your market research beforehand.

Know Your Media Formats

Now that we've covered almost all of the popular channels, I want to spend a little time talking about the formats of media. Marketing communication is essentially delivered in these 4 basic forms - text, image, video and audio. No matter what channel you use, your output will always be in these 4 formats. Now that you know, when you are planning your campaign concept - always think about your campaign key visual and key video. Every successful campaign has at least a key visual. The more successful campaigns usually have a key visual and a key video to drive the campaign. You may ask what is a key visual or a key video? It is essentially the tip of the spear, it's your weapon, it carries your key message to your target audience. Think about any Marvel movies, before any movie goes up in the theatre, a huge marketing campaign will take place to promote the movie. Generally, you will start seeing the poster and the trailer about the upcoming movie across multiple channels. It shows up on your social media feed, Youtube pre-roll, posters on billboards around the cities, you hear it on the radio, and more. The poster is essentially the key visual while the trailer is the key video. If the poster is nice, what do you do? You are more likely to watch the movie because you are captivated by it. If the trailer is exciting, what do you do? You will be very likely to watch the movie when the movie is released. Get the idea? If you need another example, Apple's flagship iPhone is a great example. Every new iPhone will have its own poster and trailer with a key tagline every time. So, the key is to always have at least one key visual or key video to spearhead your campaign.

Paid, Earn and Own Channels

Now, here's another quick short topic I want to cover before we go into full tactical planning. Paid channels are pretty straight forward - any platforms you can buy into is considered a paid channel. Now, not all channels have to be paid for. For example, if you have a prototype gadget that the world has never seen before, you probably have a very compelling story, you can pitch the opportunity to some media and they would be more than happy to write the story for you for free if you let them have a play at it. Now you just earned yourself some free coverage for your prototype product. See how that works? You can do the same thing to influencers as well. Own channels are pretty much your own platforms. It's cheaper to publish content on your own website or social media. It's cheaper to blast email to your own email list. With all that being said, leverage is the key word for this section. Try to leverage as many earn and own channels possible. Now, many people tend to get the wrong idea here, leveraging your earned and own channels does not mean not spending on these channels. The reason you leverage on earn and own channels is mainly to reduce cost. Imagine 10 paid activities vs 6 paid activities, 2 earned and 2 owned channels. The cost can be significantly reduced.

Tactical Planning

With all of that being said, you're probably wondering how you can go about setting up a tactical plan for your campaign. It's important to understand that when it comes to tactics, they are going to be the finer details. Remember that strategy we had looked at, closer to end of chapter 8 and at the "Understand The Landscape" section from above? Well, think of that strategy as your skeleton and think of your tactics as the flesh that covers that skeleton. They are the itinerary plan, or map. They make your strategy an actionable item.

Now, every tactic has a mechanic, or mechanism. The mechanism speaks to your approach and processes. You may have the very same video, for example, that you are ready to roll out on several platforms, but depending on the platform, it will be shared differently. The mechanics of it will be different for each platform. Terms and conditions on each platform are different, the recommended amount of copy or post information will be different - there are just so many varying mechanics that are in play for that very same piece of content depending on where you're planning to share it.

Tactics help you to put everything into perspective in terms of these mechanics, but they also help you to break up your strategy into small milestones that you can keep track of. For instance, working with a certain influencer will guarantee you a certain number of views by a certain date. Once the deal is signed with them, you know that there is a milestone in place that you can reach by working with them.

Your details, mechanics and milestones make up the small steps that you take towards your strategy. Try to draft your tactical roadmap by answering some core questions:

- What is the objective of this tactic?
- What is the goal of this tactic?
- What is the mechanic of this tactic?
- How does this mechanic work?
- What is the CTA, or call to action, for this tactic?
- What channels will I be using?
- How much of my budget am I planning to spend on this tactic?

Once you have the answers clearly laid out in front of you, you'll know the direction that you're taking with your tactics. It's all about being prepared and setting the correct expectations. At the end of the day, whether you are a new entrepreneur, or a seasoned one, marketing is all about convincing the next person of what you are pitching to them. You could be pitching to a customer, a new supplier, and influencer, or just about anyone else in your business sphere. Having your goals, objectives, and tactics clearly defined means that you have a script in place to sell yourself. This is the only way to sell, to pitch, and to get the results that you're after.

Just jumping ahead a little, you may be wondering how to calculate your sales goals? I'm sure many of you want to drive sales. Great! My Campaign Mastery Codex template, which encompasses ROAS calculation, is the method that I always use to calculate how to achieve my sales goals profitably. We're going to explore that part towards the end of this book, so sit tight for those details.

Putting a Tactical Overview Together

When you put a tactical overview together, there are a few elements that you want to make sure you have captured. Firstly, be specific on the channel that you are using. Have an overarching objective and an overarching goal. I also refer to these as a 'Big Objective', and a 'Big Goal', respectively. You then have a subsequent specific objective and goal which helps you work towards the mechanics, requirements, timeline, and budget.

Consider using a table like the one below.

Channel	
Big Objective	
Objective	
Big Goal	
Goal	
Mechanics	i.
	ii.
Requirements	i.
	ii.
Timeline	
Budget	

Setting a Tactical Budget & Measuring your Campaign Progress

You need to have a plan to monitor and evaluate, you may decide every three days, or even every day, to see what your numbers are each day. Go through your funnel for each channel and be granular because that is the only way to optimize. Here's a list of question that is great for optimization, start with:

- What's the spend so far?
- How many "Impression" did we get for this spend?
- How many "Reach" did we get for this spend?
- How many "Lead" did we get for this spend?
- How many "Add to Cart" for this spend?
- How many "Purchase" for this spend?

These are some good starting point. You may have very different sets of questions to ask depending on your business requirement. But generally, it shouldn't be far from this.

As an entrepreneur you need to consistently do these progress updates. Check in on your daily social engagement, and all the moving elements that are in play. How are people reacting to the posts? Continuously look for insights. See what needs changing and what needs to be held on to. I've seen so many people make the same mistake by giving up after going in on something for a few days. They gave up because they "think" the tactic is not working because they are not getting conversions "instantly". And, they rule out that the tactic does not work. The way I see it is that they have no plan on how to improve the situation. They're afraid to hold their position and it means all of the work that they've put in leading up to that moment has been for nothing. So, here's an important lesson, not getting results immediately doesn't mean it's a bad result, it's important to know what questions to ask and knowing how to measure your results. You must develop the grit to keep going. Consistency will get you there.

Probably heard this before - "Never invest everything in one pot", so to speak. In other words, don't put all of your eggs in one basket. Spread your tactics out so that you can work on a big picture. That way if one really doesn't end up working out, you can change it out and fall back on the others. Just keep progressing. At the beginning focus on the progress, not the results. Then review, improve, and keep track. What didn't work for you in the beginning might work for you later on. It's all about that progress.

The most important thing to remember, with whichever route you plan on taking in terms of tactics, always plan ahead. Knowing your goal will also be able to guide you in terms of which avenues would be better suited to achieving your goal. Knowing your budget and desires for revenue will inform your ad spend and your traffic targets. Last but not least, focus on people, in everything that you do. It is the customers, after all, who will make or break your campaign.

CHAPTER 9: RECAP
Exercise That Mental Muscle

1. Why do businesses with great products fail to pull in the numbers?

   _____

   _____

2. What is the new 'cold-calling'?

   _____

   _____

3. What is the gift you give to your customers when you engage in email marketing?

   _____

   _____

4. How should you personalize communiques?

   _____

   _____

5. Is SMS marketing a cheaper alternative?

   _____

   _____

6. Will content marketing be relevant in a post-pandemic world, and why?

_____

_____

7. What is affiliate marketing?

_____

_____

8. What is influencer marketing?

_____

_____

9. What should you take into account before going about a video marketing campaign?

_____

_____

10. How can you increase your search rankings?

_____

_____

11. What is pay-per-click marketing?

_____

_____

12. How often should you check on your campaign progress?

_____

_____

Give it your best, and head to the end for the answers.

Chapter 10:

Know your Deliverable

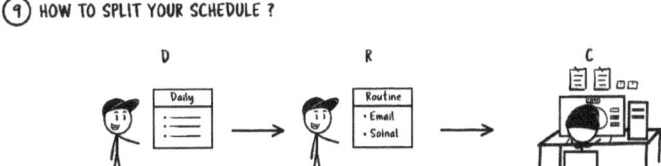

Campaign Planning

Have you set realistic timelines?

We've already spoken quite extensively about goal setting, knowing your financial targets, and strategic benchmarks, but we haven't delved into the deliverable. Are you actually able to deliver the sales numbers that you are aiming for? Do you have the production capacity to deliver within a realistic timeframe? A quick and easy death to any business would be to oversell a product or service and fail on the delivery. Further than that, the backlash can actually land you in legal and financial 'hot water', so to speak.

First off, have a look at your daily routine. This is going to determine a lot about your marketing timeline. The not-so-exciting tasks that form the bigger part of your marketing picture will have to be taken into consideration before you set any kind of marketing timeline in place. They're not just going to go away because you have an upcoming deadline. Be sure that when you set goals in terms of actual product delivery and campaign delivery, that you have sufficient time to handle your daily routine and the additional workload. You've just got to be realistic.

You don't want to end up feeling burnt out or working counterintuitively. Having a realistic timeline is such an important factor in how quickly you can turn a project around. You need to be working towards a clearly defined goal. If you're not then you're going to be providing a substandard level of work with little direction.

I want you to think about the level of work that you expect yourself to put out, while we're on the subject. Wanting to create lengthy copy in the same amount of time that it takes for you to create Facebook copy is just insanity. Think carefully about the medium, or platform, that you're using for your campaigns and then break it down on how long it should take. Work out an hourly or daily word count target and factor in the other not-so-exciting tasks we spoke of earlier.

You need to create schedules and calendars for all of the upcoming campaigns that you're working on. If you can create a virtual calendar then you'll be in a position to see whether or not you can actually complete the tasks by the deadline. Segment your marketing strategies and create micro deadlines for varying facets of content driven campaigns.

It's true that the quicker you can deliver, the quicker you can start seeing increments in sales revenue, but you can't rush the process. It is wholly unfair to yourself to place unnecessary amounts of pressure on the process. You'll most likely end up delivering a substandard product or service that leaves a bad taste in your customers' mouths. When you take the time to plan your campaigns under realistic timelines, you can build up a hype around your product launch and really get off to a great start. You can consciously plan for growth and for success, without the pressure of running around to meet crazy deadlines in the midnight hour.

Let your timeline flow throughout your entire business. The marketing deadlines should correlate with the accounting deadlines, which should correlate with the administrative deadlines. If you've got a product launch or new campaign coming up, follow these steps in order to ensure that you're on track and on schedule.

Keep it real

Don't take shots in the dark, ask a professional. If you have no idea how much time goes into creating 2,500-word copy, then ask the person who you are delegating to how much time they think they would need in order to get the job done. This is, of course, if you have someone assisting you with this or if you are hiring a third-party to work with you on a specific campaign.

The best way to get off the ground with a bang is to have the right support on board from the start. Besides, it's one less thought process off your plate, and you get to give as much attention to your sales process as possible.

Stay in your lane

You need your support system to know the role that they're going to be playing in the grand scheme of things. Not only should they know their role, they should have specific and measurable targets that they need to reach; broken down into micro-deadlines. Set milestones such as first draft, sign-off, approval, roll out, and so on.

Prioritize like a Jedi

Find out what the main goal is, and work from a principle of fundamentals in order to solve any problems that could be in the way of that goal. When you get down to the bare basics, you'll be able to define which of the deliverables are more important than others, and which are just icing on the cake. When you have that clear image in mind, it's easier for you to prioritize the most important elements and trim the fat off in terms of the wasteful or less-important ones.

Let your timeline be reflective of the prioritized elements and have them set out, in order, right up until the point of final completion. Leave nothing to chance. Not only are you going to be saving on precious resources such as time and money, but you're also going to be encouraging yourself along the way. You'll begin to feel as though you are only working on tasks of high-importance, and you will excel in light of this.

Overall, your timelines need to be just like your goals, specific, measurable, attainable, relevant and time-bound. Time is of the essence; quite literally. Be sure that you are being realistic with the expectations you have of yourself. Don't be afraid to consult where your knowledge is lacking and be sure to stay on course with your calendar.

Once you've reached a point where your timelines are harmoniously orchestrated and well-balance, you can begin setting greater campaign targets and planning your marketing tactics for ultimate success.

CHAPTER 10: RECAP
Exercise That Mental Muscle

1. What is a sales deliverable?

   _____

   _____

2. What is a campaign deliverable?

   _____

   _____

3. What should you create in order to keep upcoming campaigns on track?

   _____

   _____

4. What steps can you take to make sure a product launch is on track?

   _____

   _____

Give it your best, and head to the end for the answers.

Chapter 11:

The ROAS to Hell is Paved with Good Intentions

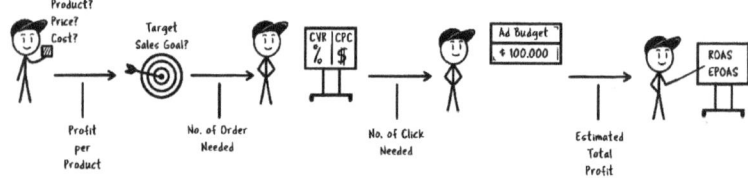

Gauge Your Success

Everyone wants to know what their ROI, or return on investment, is but they hardly ever break it down to something that is crucial to successfully adjusting your strategy in terms of campaigns; their ROAS, or return on ad spend. Yes, online advertisements offer you a range of affordable avenues, and you can tailor your campaigns to suit your budget, but you don't want to be just throwing that money away do you? In order for you to reach that $1,000,000 target; you are going to have to know your ROAS in order to optimize the scaling of your business.

This isn't just important for you to know whether or not you're wasting your marketing budget, it's important for you to know whether you're engaging and converting your target audience at the right channels. Is your message working? Which channel is giving you better ROAS? At the end, the most crucial question is whether your campaign is generating enough return for you?

Being able to calculate your ROAS is going to help you in deciding what is your next best step to take for your campaign in order to optimize and maximize your return. If you haven't been running this calculation all along, how do you know if any of your paid advertisements are really performing? The answer is, you don't.

I'm going to keep this chapter short and sweet because I want the impact of the message to be as concentrated as possible. Furthermore, I want you to move on to some other key metrics that you need to undertake in order to measure and find out the results of your marketing efforts.

Ready?

Let's get to it!

Example #1

You spend $1,000 on YouTube Ads promoting a product.

You get 30,000 video views and $2,000 from selling a product from your website through the video link.

Your ROAS is 2x

i.e. $2,000 ÷ $1,000 = 2x

Your ROI is 100% at $1,000 Profit + 30,000 video views is a bonus metrics for awareness.

Example #2

You spend $1,200 on Facebook Ads promoting your courses.

You get 300 Likes, 30 Shares and $3,600 from 3 new course students.

Your ROAS is 3x

i.e. $3,600 ÷ $1,200 = 3x

Your ROI is 200% at $2,400 + 300 Likes + 30 Shares as a bonus metrics for awareness.

Example #3

You spend $12,000 on all digital ads to promote your program.

You get 200 Leads and $60,000 from 5 sign ups.

Your ROAS is 5x

i.e. $60,000 ÷ $12,000 = 5x

Your ROI is 400% at $48,000 + 200 Leads as potential bonus sales metrics for follow up

You'll notice that I've added in the leads, likes, shares and video views as a return on investment. This is because it can be near impossible to calculate how many of your video views turned into sales, unless there was a direct path followed from a link in the video to a landing page. Moreover, you want to take this as a return on investment as videos with high watch counts, or views, will inevitably generate a buzz around your product. The comments section will quickly tell you whether that buzz is good or bad.

Leads are obviously a good return on investment because even those that are not quite ready for the purchasing process can always be nurtured or kept 'warm' to pitch further products and services to later. Any amount of data in the way of potential customers' personal information is a win in my book, as long as they can be used to generate revenue at some point.

Likes and shares are going to grow your following, which means even though your customer might not be the one who viewed the video, their engagement with it could direct it towards someone on their friend's or following's list who is.

Take this and run with it! It is a simple, foolproof, calculation that I use consistently for any campaign that I want to spend precious ad bucks on. It will allow you to make quick comparisons and keep you abreast of whether or not your efforts are generating the revenue that you need in order to justify the spend.

If you want to get into the finer details of it all, you can use my very own Campaign Master Codex calculator. This is especially good to get an in-depth understanding of the results on particular ad campaigns.

Given all of the data that you can get out of platforms, they can help you to target even the audience that you want to reach with pinpoint accuracy. Due to the technology that we have today, we are able to do these insanely accurate predictions.

You want to get to EPROAS, or your estimated profit return on ad spend. Bear in mind that when you're working on these calculations you shouldn't average your fixed asset costs in your product cost area. Now let's use a simple example here. Say you're going to make, or source, a pencil and you're going to be selling this product. Hypothesize that the cost to make it is $3, and you are going to sell it for $30. Your gross profit is then $27.

One of the questions I get asked a lot is how much should I spend on ads. My answer is always the same. You should first focus on how much you want to make and then calculate backwards to figure out how much you want to spend. Let's say you want to make a gross profit of $27,000. How many pencils do you need to sell? More importantly, what are the gross sales that you need to make in order to reach that amount? If I wanted to make a total gross profit of $27,000 dollars, I would need to divide this by my gross profit per item; or $27. $27,000 / $27 = 1,000 pieces. Now what would my gross sales need to be? 1,000 pieces x $30 sales price = $30,000. My total cost to manufacture all 1,000 pencils would be $3,000. Pretty straight forward math, right?

Next up is the most important step. This is where we talk about ads and conversion rates. Your conversion rate will always be worked out as a percentage. 1% conversion is the general rule of thumb when it comes to ad targeting on any digital ad platforms.. At 1% conversion rate, you will need 100,000 clicks to get 1,000 orders. CPC might cost you $0.10; which is generally low.

Your CPC will be higher if you're selling something more valuable or complicated. However, if you're aiming for brand awareness with an 'everyday-buy' or 'every day-use' product, also known as a mass product, your targeting will be more general which means your CPC will be lower. If you're selling something that is more niche focused and that requires more intense targeting and retargeting strategy, then your initial CPC is expected to be higher. We may want to look at cost per lead (CPL) or cost per acquisition (CPA) to get a better picture of the conversion rate at each level through the funnel. But with all that being said, if you do not have an existing email list with purchase value or lead list, it all comes down to getting that first batch of data of traffic and optimizing it over time with custom audience targeting as you go deeper.

So, in this case of the pencil, let's use CPC of $0.10, you need to spend $10,000 on ads in order to generate 1,000 sales. From the $27,000 gross profit, your estimated net profit after ad spend would be $17,000; i.e. $27,000 minus $10,000. Your ROAS will be 3 times your amount on ad spend and your EPROAS will be 1.7 times your amount on ad spend. That's quite a decent amount.

This is very important: watch your cost per click! The more your cost per click, the less your EPROAS will be. Of course, with the right strategies and retargeting, your conversion rate could increase depending on certain factors, and that will of course increase your EPROAS. It's all simple mathematics, and everything is linked together.

PRODUCT		CAMPAIGN DURATION	DAILY	TRACK YOUR PROGRESS		20	DAYS
Step 1: Calculate Your Profit Per Product		Duration Ratio (%)	5%	25%	50%	75%	100%
Product Price ($)	30	Campaign Ratio (Days)	1	5	10	15	20
Product Cost ($)	3						
Profit Per Product ($)	27						
Step 2: Set Your Sales Goal							
Gross Profit ($)	27,000	Gross Profit ($)	1,350	6,750	13,500	20,250	27,000
No. of Orders	1,000	No. of Orders	50	250	500	750	1,000
Gross Sales ($)	30,000	Gross Sales ($)	1,500	7,500	15,000	22,500	30,000
Gross Cost	3,000	Gross Cost	150	750	1,500	2,250	3,000
Step 3: Set Your Conversion Rate							
Conversion (%)	1.0%	Conversion (%)	1.0%	1.0%	1.0%	1.0%	1.0%
No. of Clicks Needed	100,000	No. of Clicks Needed	5,000	25,000	50,000	75,000	100,000
Step 4: Set Your Cost Per Click							
Cost Per Click ($)	0.10	Cost Per Click ($)	0.20	0.10	0.10	0.10	0.10
Ad Spend Needed	10,000	Ad Spend Needed	1,000	2,500	5,000	7,500	10,000
Step 5: Estimated Net Profit & ROAS							
Estimated Net Profit	17,000	Estimated Net Profit	350	4,250	8,500	12,750	17,000
ROAS (X)	3.0	ROAS (X)	1.5	3.0	3.0	3.0	3.0
EPROAS (X)	1.70	EPROAS (X)	0.35	1.70	1.70	1.70	1.70

Now, when it comes to digital products, you have a lot more potential for a higher EPROAS. This is simply because your product cost in comparison to a physical product is going to be a lot lower. Webinars, online courses, and digital services amongst many others have the potential to skyrocket your EPROAS. Here, we assume that your product cost is zero because even annual subscriptions to platforms like Zoom, and so on, will be annual and averaged out. Have a look below.

PRODUCT			TRACK YOUR PROGRESS				
Step 1: Calculate Your Profit Per Product		CAMPAIGN DURATION	DAILY	1	/	20	DAYS
Product Price ($)	4,997	Duration Ratio (%)	5%	25%	50%	75%	100%
Product Cost ($)							
Profit Per Product ($)	4,997	Campaign Ratio (Days)	1	5	10	15	20
Step 2: Set Your Sales Goal							
Gross Profit ($)	100,000	Gross Profit ($)	5,000	25,000	50,000	75,000	100,000
No. of Orders	20	No. of Orders	1	5	10	15	20
Gross Sales ($)	100,000	Gross Sales ($)	5,000	25,000	50,000	75,000	100,000
Gross Cost	0	Gross Cost	0	0	0	0	0
Step 3: Set Your Conversion Rate							
Conversion (%)	1.0%	Conversion (%)	1.0%	1.0%	1.0%	1.0%	1.0%
No. of Clicks Needed	2,001	No. of Clicks Needed	100	500	1,001	1,501	2,001
Step 4: Set Your Cost Per Click							
Cost Per Click ($)	10.00	Cost Per Click ($)	0.20	10.00	10.00	10.00	10.00
Ad Spend Needed	20,012	Ad Spend Needed	20	5,003	10,006	15,009	20,012
Step 5: Estimated Net Profit & ROAS							
Estimated Net Profit	79,988	Estimated Net Profit	4,980	19,997	39,994	59,991	79,988
ROAS (X)	5.0	ROAS (X)	249.9	5.0	5.0	5.0	5.0
EPROAS (X)	4.00	EPROAS (X)	249.85	4.00	4.00	4.00	4.00

When it comes to digital products, the average CPC is going to be around $5 - $7. This is a great place to peg your CPC because it ensures more refined targeting. The higher end regarding digital products would be around $10 and above.

Before this digital age, advertising was often based on speculation numbers. You'd think of how many people are actively buying the newspaper that you're advertising in. Now that we have tons of accurate data, it's easy to make money from little advertising investment. With this example above, we can say that your ad might get shown hundreds of thousands of times. The number of people who actually see it will be in the tens of thousands; and 2,001 people will have decided to click on it. With EPROAS at 4 times your return on ad spend, that's an insane achievement!

Creating a Best- and Worst-Case Scenario

Try to create 3 scenarios from best case to worst case so that you know whether or not you're in the clear in terms of

EPROAS on all scenarios. The best-case scenario is going to let you know just how much you can achieve. Your worst-case scenario is going to let you know if you're venturing dangerously low in terms of profit, and what you can do in terms of ad spend to combat this.

SCENARIO 1		SCENARIO 2		SCENARIO 3	
PRODUCT		**PRODUCT**		**PRODUCT**	
Step 1: Calculate Your Profit Per Product		Step 1: Calculate Your Profit Per Product		Step 1: Calculate Your Profit Per Product	
Product Price ($)	7	Product Price ($)	7	Product Price ($)	7
Product Cost ($)		Product Cost ($)		Product Cost ($)	
Profit Per Product ($)	7	Profit Per Product ($)	7	Profit Per Product ($)	7
Step 2: Set Your Sales Goal		Step 2: Set Your Sales Goal		Step 2: Set Your Sales Goal	
Gross Profit ($)	5,000	Gross Profit ($)	5,000	Gross Profit ($)	5,000
No. of Orders	714	No. of Orders	714	No. of Orders	714
Gross Sales ($)	5,000	Gross Sales ($)	5,000	Gross Sales ($)	5,000
Gross Cost	0	Gross Cost	0	Gross Cost	0
Step 3: Set Your Conversion Rate		Step 3: Set Your Conversion Rate		Step 3: Set Your Conversion Rate	
Conversion (%)	5.0%	Conversion (%)	4.0%	Conversion (%)	3.0%
No. of Clicks Needed	14,286	No. of Clicks Needed	17,857	No. of Clicks Needed	23,810
Step 4: Set Your Cost Per Click		Step 4: Set Your Cost Per Click		Step 4: Set Your Cost Per Click	
Cost Per Click ($)	0.10	Cost Per Click ($)	0.10	Cost Per Click ($)	0.10
Ad Spend Needed	1,429	Ad Spend Needed	1,786	Ad Spend Needed	2,381
Step 5: Estimated Net Profit & ROAS		Step 5: Estimated Net Profit & ROAS		Step 5: Estimated Net Profit & ROAS	
Estimated Net Profit	3,571	Estimated Net Profit	3,214	Estimated Net Profit	2,619
ROAS (X)	3.5	ROAS (X)	2.8	ROAS (X)	2.1
EPROAS (X)	2.50	EPROAS (X)	1.80	EPROAS (X)	1.10

EPROAS is a bonus that is usually used by professionals in the business – people who know about it. Action budget setting is what you should focus on if you're starting out as an entrepreneur and want to get ahead of the game in terms of your campaigns.

A&P spend happens on a daily basis, and that's why I choose to look at my progress on a daily basis. As such, this is also why I recommend it for you. Try to work on a budget setting table such as the one below to get a good grip of what you're working with. It's a lot simpler than the previous tables and it will get your foot in the door in terms of your progress evaluation if you're a fairly new entrepreneur, or looking for a simple solution to assess your ROAS.

Example:

No.	Tactics	A&P Spend ($)	Revenue	ROAS
1	Digital Acquisition			

2	PR Influencer Launch			
3	Daily Social Post			
4	Weekly Videos			
5	Monthly Reports			
6	Yearly Conference			
7	Website Costing			
	Total:			

We've already looked at return on ad spend, or ROAS, as well as estimated profit return on ad spend, or EPROAS, now it's time to go back to basics and look at your return on investment, or ROI. Working out your return on investment in terms of a specific ad campaign is pretty effortless. You just have to minus the overall costs to run the campaign from the overall revenue generated.

Dollar Value Example

$2,400 on ad spend

$3,900 in overall revenue as a direct conversion to sales generated by the ad

ROI = $1,500

    i.e. $3,900 - $2,400 = $1,500

Percentage Value Example

(Sales Growth - Marketing Cost) ÷ Marketing Cost = ROI

OR

Net return on investment   x 100%

    Cost of investment

Following the above example's figures:

$$\frac{(\$3900-\$2400)}{\$2400} \times 100\% = 62.49\%$$

Other than your ROI, you'll also want to work out your cost per lead. A part of measuring your success is not only measuring your returns, but find outing your costs. For this case, we won't consider the quality of leads such as marketing qualified and sales qualified leads, but we'll focus on the broader spectrum of the word 'lead'.

Cost Per Lead Example

Campaign budget = $2,400

Total leads generated = 20

$$\frac{\text{Campaign budget}}{\text{Total Leads}} = \$120$$

You cost per lead was $120. This is not going to be a very efficient CPL if each lead brings in a sale under that value. Weigh up your CPL in terms of revenue generated as a result.

With leads in mind, let's move on to your conversion rate. When you spend precious resources on marketing campaigns, you want to know what the conversion rate was.

Conversion Rate Example

Number of visitors to your site as a result of an ad campaign = 1,500

Leads generated = 20

$$\frac{\text{Leads generated}}{\text{Number of visitors}} \times 100\% = 1.3\%$$

Your conversion rate is 1.3%

Your cost per sale differs slightly from your cost per lead in that it highlights how much each sale cost you as opposed to each lead. This number will be significantly higher since your actual sales will be lower than your leads.

Cost Per Acquisition Example

Number of sales = 10

Campaign budget = $2,400

Campaign budget = $240
Number of sales

Factor in how much you received as a result of each sale in order to work out the possible profit margin.

Finally, we reach the incremental sales. These measure the overall sales in conjunction with specific campaigns. This will allow you to find out which of your campaigns are generating more sales revenue for you by comparison to others.

Incremental Sales Example

Overall sales for the month = $450,000

Total sales from the campaign = $3,900

Campaign Sales   x 100% = 0.87%
Monthly sales

Your campaign contributed 0.87% to your total sales revenue for the month.

If the campaign sapped up a lot of your time and energy, consider it against other campaigns which may have generated a higher percentage. Find out the strengths and weaknesses of both and plan a strategy to optimize them.

Knowing where you stand in terms of your costs and returns will allow you to make smarter choices in terms of marketing budgets and campaign planning.

CHAPTER 11: RECAP
Exercise That Mental Muscle

1. What is ROI?

   _____

   _____

2. What is ROAS?

   _____

   _____

3. Can you factor in other gains, other than financial, into your ROI?

   _____

   _____

4. How do you work out your ROAS?

   _____

   _____

5. What is EPROAS?

   _____

   _____

6. What is the rule of thumb conversion rate for platforms like Facebook?

7. How do you work out your ROI?

8. What is cost-per-lead?

9. How do you work out cost-per-lead?

10. What is conversion rate?

11. How do you work out your conversion rate?

12. What is cost-per-sale?

13. How do you work out your cost-per-sale?

14. How do you work out your incremental sales?

_____

_____

Give it your best, and head to the end for the answers.

Chapter 12:

BONUS!

Making your Money Work for you
&
5 Step Money Making Formula for Digital Ads

I used to be the type of person who would just spend without thinking. It's a terrible trap to fall into, especially for a business. Here's a little-known secret, you don't have to utilize every single marketing resource out there, constantly, in order to achieve financial success. You just have to figure out what works best for you. Trial and error, with a whole lot of performance measurement is the perfect way to do this. As a marketer or entrepreneur, it's your job to generate a marketing buzz around your product; you now know exactly how to do it, so don't fall into a loop of spending on campaigns frivolously if they're not benefiting you, or if you don't really need to.

If you're just starting out in your own venture, then you need to cultivate the will power to say 'no'. Don't be miserly; be spendthrift. Spend where you need to, and save where you can. You need to be able to accumulate enough capital to reinvest into your business and more importantly into valuable marketing avenues. The more you spend needlessly, the less funds you will have aside to scale your business and launch great campaigns. There's no correct percentage that you should be spending or saving, it's all about control. Controlling your budget, your spending habits and your cash flow, gives you more buying power in the long run.

Don't confuse spending money with making money. Spending money is when you part with money with no avenue for it come back to you. Making money is when you part with money with the intention for it to return to you at a greater value. In my opinion, every time you spend money, it should have a return. You have to decide what you want to get back and how much you're willing to spend to get it.

That being said, none of us are perfect. We all make mistakes along the way. I'll tell you right now, nothing worth having will ever come easy. My number 1 secret to learning how to control your cash flow, is to make as many relatively small financial mistakes, and make them relatively quickly. Try not to kill your credit in the process. We're talking mistakes here, not life re-setting cataclysms.

Think about it logically; when you make a mistake, you know exactly how not to make that same mistake again, don't you? Trial and error. I learnt how to manage my money and my marketing budgets because I was frivolous in my younger years. I often refer to that time as the quarter of a million-dollar learning curve; I figure that's how much I had burnt through by the time the financial bell rang over my head. There is no better teacher than your own mistakes, but err with caution. You're heading into business to make a profit. You're employing people, including yourself; don't leave everyone unemployed. Don't let yourself down, if you can help it. Don't plan to fail, but embrace a certain level of mistakes.

If anyone had to ask me what my 3 rules to financial success are, I would say:

Rule #1 - Do not be afraid to make any money mistakes.

Rule #2 - If you make a mistake, tell yourself "It's ok", try not to repeat it, and move on.

Rule #3 - If you make the same mistake again, refer to Rule #2 and don't make a big fuss about it.

Embrace it.

Take the hardships as a sign of growth; roll with the punches. You need to develop a gritty mentality in order to hack it in any business. If you can build up your tolerance for mistakes then you will eventually come out on top. As long as you don't give up, you will succeed. I truly believe in that statement.

When it comes to learning how to control your cash flow, be patient with yourself. Learn the metrics that I've provided. Make sound, rational decisions based on you campaign performance and reinvest in areas where you are getting positive results.

At the end of the day money-making is all about managing your time, your mind and your tolerance levels.

With all of the knowledge I have already given you, if you really want to control that cash flow, then you should:

1. Find out your profitability;
2. Draw up a cash flow projection; and,
3. Speed up your income or inflows.

You have the tools to do it now. What are you waiting for?

I want to leave you with a bonus; my 5-step money making formula for digital ads. I've shown you how to measure the success of your own campaigns, but now I'm going to show you 5 simple steps that generate tons of revenue, in a fraction of the time.

It simply comes down to making predictive calculations and being committed to seeing them through.

Step #1

Identify your product price and cost to determine your profit.

Product Price = $100

Product Cost = $20

Profit/Unit = $80 (Product Price - Product Cost)

It is important to know your profit before you attempt to proceed to the next step.

Step #2

Set your sales goal to determine the number of orders you need to sell and your profit.

Sales Goal: $10,000

Total Product Cost: $2,000

Orders Needed: 100 units (Sales Goal / Product Price)

Step #3

Set an estimated conversion rate range, or CVR, to determine the number of clicks you need.

CVR (%) = 1%

Clicks Needed = 10,000 (Orders Needed / 1%)

It is critical to set a conversion rate that reflects closest to your industry or competition average.

Take into consideration the fact that setting an inaccurate rate may result in incorrect estimations, thus giving yourself false expectations. If you cannot work out a benchmark, 1% should always be your minimum conversion rate.

Once you start your first campaign, you can benchmark the data from there.

Step #4

Set an estimated cost per click, or CPC, to determine the amount that you need to spend.

CPC= $0.20

Spend Needed= $2,000 (Clicks Needed x CPC)

Just as with your CVR, it is critical to set a cost per click that reflects your industry or competition average.

If you cannot work out a benchmark, $0.20 should always be your minimum rate.

Step #5

Calculate your profit and return on ad spend (ROAS)

Net Profit= $6,000 (Sales Goal - Total Product Cost - Spend Needed)

ROAS (X)= 5x (Sales Goal / Spend Needed)

EPROAS (X)= 3x (Estimated Profit / Spend Needed)

Knowing your EPROAS, or Estimated Profit Return on Ad Spend, will let you know whether you are actually making a profit or loss. Sometimes when your product cost is too high, even if you have a decent ROAS, you may have a negative EPROAS which means you are actually making a loss.

How simple is that? 5 quick steps with 5 easy to grasp formulas to get you started.

Now, get out there, and start making some positive changes to your marketing strategies. If you get stuck, come back to this book for inspiration and keep marching on.

Best of luck for the campaign ahead!

CHAPTER 12: RECAP
Exercise That Mental Muscle

1. What do you need to cultivate in terms of cash-flow early on?

   _____
   _____

2. What are the key differences between spending money frivolously and spending money as an investment?

   _____
   _____

3. What are 3 rules surrounding money mistakes?

   _____
   _____

4. How can you control your cash flow?

   _____
   _____

Give it your best, and head to the end for the answers.

Parting Advice from the Author

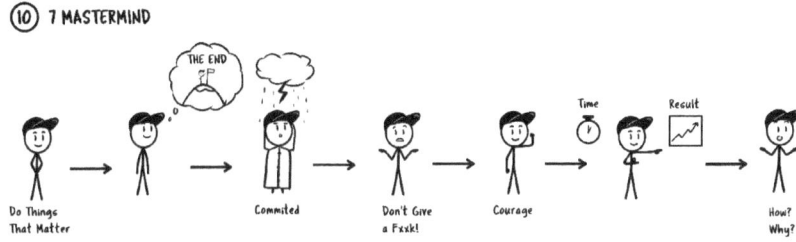

Do the things that matter

Make sure that whatever you do in this life is meaningful and impactful. Contribute to the overall benefit of the population. Make a difference. Solve a problem. Don't waste your time or your life, doing something that doesn't matter to you.

Start with the end in mind

Visualize the end goal. What does success look like to you? What is the best outcome from point A to point B. Start with that point B and work your way back to figure out what you need to do to get there? That vision will drive you to continue to learn and progress.

Commitment

Early on in our lives, as young people, commitment is just not something in the books. You need to learn to commit. Live through the journey; the highs and lows. Have the consistency and the mindset to see things through. When you have commitment, you will have the energy to move forward. Success is not about having all the nice things; it's about making things happen at a grassroots level. When you make things happen at that level, the bigger things will come and fall into place. Commitment is the driver for consistency.

Don't give a f*ck

You will meet all kinds of people in your life. People who are cheats, and enemies in disguise. You will even get people in your own family who look down on you. You'll come across people with agendas. Try not to care about them. Focus on the people who share the same goals and passion as you. Anyone who has the mentality that they are a boss and you have to run circles around them can either say nice things to you to get what they want, or nasty things to piss you off. Smile and walk it off. Don't take anything to heart, good or bad. Don't let the good things go to your head, and don't let bad things get to your heart. Don't let people affect you!

How & Why

Ask lots of 'whys' and 'hows'. Why are we doing something? How are we doing it? The reasons why you're doing something will help you to monitor your progress. Put an interest into whatever you are doing. Be curious and be aware of the things happening around you. It's going to help you to align with people who are working with you. Ask questions along the way. It's a preliminary filter that you should use to avoid petty arguments due to misunderstandings.

Time & Result

Both are equally important, but there is a lot of prioritization to do in terms of each. Business is a constant play of moving parts. Some things need time to see results. Some things need immediate results. Do the things that need immediate results first. Just do it. Don't hesitate. Have your eye on the details, to make sure that when you're rolling these immediate efforts out that there aren't any mess ups.

Courage

It's important in everything that you do. You have to have the guts to go after something. You have to be willing to make tough decisions. There is only so much time you have, so you need to be clear of mind and brave enough to pull the trigger even when things are not 100% ready. Perfectionism is for the professional fields; engineers, and doctors need to give 100%. Entrepreneurs need to have the courage to go with 90%. We have the leeway to play around and play things by ear in order to make things happen - and happen fast. Things will go wrong. It's inevitable. Have the courage to foresee the problems and run with them.

Most of all – this is your life. Live it. Embrace it. Have fun!

SUMMARY OF CONCEPTS

We started off this journey to marketing campaign success with branding. By now, you should know that establishing a good brand with great value perception is the first stop on your road to success. The public are the ones who are buying into what you're selling, so your public image has to be on point. Look at everything from your brand colors, to your logo, your tone and even the perceived personality of your brand. People don't just buy products; they buy *into* brands.

It might seem pretty obvious, but you need to know what you're selling. Moreover, your customer support representatives, whether that's you or someone you've hired, need to have an intricate understanding of the product or service in order to answer any questions that a potential customer may have. An unprepared answer, makes for a loss in sales revenue.

Everyone wants to know how they can go about increasing their sales revenue, and it starts off with understanding your clients. They should feel like they are part of the family when they engage with your brand. If you set your sights on solving as many customer disputes, complaints and concerns effectively, you are going to be on to the winning streak. But don't just solve these problems to placate your customers; solve them with the intention to learn from your mistakes. You want to ensure that you're streamlining your product or service delivery and brand experience so that you have less problems to content with in future.

SUMMARY OF CONCEPTS

With the right customer service mindset, it's time to start rolling out the big guns; your DRS system. You want to hack into the potential of the internet, and utilize it to reach more people, gain insight into your customers concerns and deliver the goods in a fast manner. Say it with me; data, reach, and speed!

You'll then need to figure out where you've been missing the mark to ensure it doesn't happen again, or at least not as often, in future. Find out whether you're getting out what you're putting in. Whip out that calculator and start working on your financial goals, strategies, costs and input vs. output.

If you've noticed any problems in your current strategies you need to be able to plan objectives around them. Know what you are trying to solve, address or achieve and create action plans around the key insights.

Knowing your brand, problems and targets will allow you to properly plan your marketing campaigns. Try to pay particular attention to social media. People are constantly whiling the hours away on social media, and a well-timed, well put together post can draw in major traffic and potential leads.

When you start getting serious about your business, your marketing strategy, your campaign, you need to get even more serious about your returns. I'm not just talking about return on investment in terms of following growth and traffic generation, I want you to get specific enough to determine your return on ad spend for each and every campaign you roll out. Metrics are the only way to tell if you're on the right path, or completely missing the mark.

Overall, you should be setting realistic timelines, measuring your success and controlling your cash flow. If you can adhere to some of these simple tips, I have no doubt in my mind that this year will be your best year yet.

As long as you keep learning and growing, there's nowhere but up from here.

ANSWERS

Have a look at how you faired in terms of answering the chapter recap questions:

Chapter 1: Recap

1. What is your Brand Experience'?
   a. Brand experience refers to the thoughts and feelings that come about as a result of engaging with your brand. It is the consistent experience that customers perceive to have.

2. Why is brand experience important?
   a. It's important because it will shape how you are perceived by customers and stakeholders alike. It can drive brand loyalty.

3. List the 4 basic ways that that you can drive your brand presence.
   a. Event participation, engaging customers' senses, getting in on pop-culture, and making your approach as personal as possible.

4. What is the importance of Brand Image & Positioning?

ANSWERS

a. It will help you explore and refine the level of uniqueness that you have in the eyes of your target audience.

5. What is your brand personality?

    a. It is the human characteristics attributed to your brand.

6. Why does brand voice matter?

    a. 30% of the reason that your brand might stand out is due to its personality or voice.

7. List the 3 basic ways to develop your brand voice.

    a. Audit yourself, document how you engage with customers, get to grips with you tone.

8. What are the 10 basic brand elements?

    a. Logo, brand name, shape, tagline, color, graphics, movement, sound, taste, and smell.

9. What percentage of consumers judge a brand based on its color palette alone?

    a) 90%.

10. What are the predetermining factors in choosing a brand color palette?

    a. Your target market, the appropriateness of the color in terms of your image and message, and the ability to put it to consistent use.

11. What is the first stop on your list in terms of improving brand personality?

    a. You'll have to shape, or change, your target audience's personal opinion about your brand.

12. What is Brand Value Perception?

a. This is the value that you customer feel is derived from using your products or services.

13. Why is brand value perception important?

    a. It is a direct reflection of your target audience's perception of you and it is very difficult to change once it is cemented their minds.

Chapter 2: Recap

1. What helps products to sell like hot cakes?

    a. Your USP, or unique selling point.

2. What percentage of new businesses fail within their first 5 years of operation?

    a. 60%.

3. What do you need to focus on in your early years?

    a. Surviving before moving on to thriving.

4. List the questions that you need to ask yourself in order to benchmark your brand against the competition?

    a. What is your product?

    What exactly does your product do?

    What problem does your product solve?

    What are the benefits of your product?

    Can people live without it?

    Why should people buy it?

    Are there any other similar products in the market?

    If yes, how much do each of those products cost?

    Can this problem be solved by using any other means aside from using your product or the other similar products?

ANSWERS

   If yes, what is it and how much does it cost?

   How much are you pricing your product?

   Why is it priced at this amount?

   Would people pick up your product over all other products or other means?

5. What are the products called that serve as substitutes instead of competition to your brand?

   a. Comparative products.

Chapter 3: Recap

1. What is the number 1 question I get asked on a regular basis?

   a. "How do I increase my sales revenue?"

2. Is diversification going to help you if your current customers are dissatisfied?

   a. No. Your current customers are your top priority.

3. How do you make patron customers feel special?

   a. Offer them specials and deals that newcomers don't have access to.

4. Should you alienate newcomer customers in favor of patrons?

   a. No. Walk a middle-ground. Encourage the newcomers to become patrons so that they can get excellent rewards.

5. Is negative online feedback bad or good, and why?

   a. It can be a good thing if you use it to solve the problem, and market the fact that you are solving customers problems.

6. Should you try to speed up the communication process when you're resolving a customer service issue?

    a. No. Speed up the rate at which you respond and try to allow the customer to guide the length of the communicative window.

7. How do you go the extra mile after you've been in contact with a customer?

    a. Send out updates or get in contact afterwards to follow-up.

8. Can you release sponsored posts without a call to action?

    a. No. It's a waste of money. Try to always drive following or promote a product.

9. How many seconds do you have to stop people in their tracks as they are scrolling?

    a. 3-7 seconds.

10. How do you safeguard yourself from chancers in terms of money back guarantees?

    a. Make sure your in-house or third part legal team has all loopholes tracked, checked and covered.

11. Are reviews bad or good for public image?

    a. If you're providing quality products or services, they work wonders for your image.

12. Can you conduct product or service testing on your own, and why?

    a. I don't recommend it. You could end up with biased, question-led, answers.

ANSWERS

Chapter 4: Recap

1. What is DRS in terms of marketing?
   a. Data, reach and speed.

2. Can you achieve success online with no marketing budget?
   a. No. It is more affordable than traditional marketing but you still need to spend a little to make something out of it.

3. How has DRS leveled the playing field?
   a. It has given us all the opportunity to access far reaching target audiences; a benefit which was once only reserved for the rich.

4. What is the major cost that you will have to contend with?
   a. Your only real cost would be your internet subscription.

5. What are the 3 'unfair' advantages that DRS will give you?
   a. It will take the limits off of your possibilities, it will increase the number of resources you have, and it will unlock your access to the world.

6. How can you maintain consistency online?
   a. Post regularly and make sure that your content type is consistent as well.

7. What will happen if you are inconsistent?
   a. You will lose your customers to the competition.

8. What does transparency do for your brand?

    a. It allows your customers to make decisions about their purchases a lot faster and it allows for brand loyalty from them.

Chapter 5: Recap

1. Why are campaign goals important?

    a. Without campaign goals, you're effectively throwing money down the drain.

2. What is A/B testing?

    a. This is a process of setting up two landing pages with two similar campaigns in order to find out which of the two is more effective.

3. How will A/B testing help you campaign efforts?

    a. This ensure that you are using the most effective closing approach.

4. What are the 9 prevailing factors to take into consideration when you are find outing your campaigns?

    a. Post engagement;

       Website traffic;

       Customer retention;

       Sales;

       Brand awareness;

       Customer acquisition;

       Lead generation;

       Thought leadership; and,

       Lead nurturing.

ANSWERS

5. What are social media analytics good for?

    a. To find out which of your digital content is getting more engagement and why.

6. What are web analytics good for?

    a. To find out where people are clicking away, heavily and poorly trafficked pages, and the days of the week where you see the most traffic.

7. What should you be looking out for on your web analytics?

    a. Look at what regions most of your traffic comes from, your least and most frequented pages, the average time spent on said pages and where they click away.

Chapter 6: Recap

1. Why do people fail at marketing campaigns?

    a. This is often due to inefficient planning.

2. Are the core fundamentals of marketing the same for online and offline efforts?

    a. Yes.

3. What is the key difference between traditional marketing and digital marketing?

    a. The only key difference is the platforms which you use to deliver a campaign.

4. What is proximity convenience?

    a. This is what happens when a person picks a product because it is closer to them in terms of proximity. It's a 'first in line' train of thought.

5. How do you eliminate the proximity convenience problem?
    a. Create the notion that you are the most unique and the most beneficial brand out there.
6. What is the mistake that many businesses make when they go into a temporary decline?
    a. They shave off some of their marketing efforts.
7. What are the more likely reasons for a temporary decline?
    a. External factors such as an economic downturn.
8. What are the 7 core fundamentals of marketing?
    a. Product, Price, Place, Promotion, Customer, Competitor, and Environment.
9. Why will the deliberation of fundamentals vary across competitors?
    a. Because we all view the fundamentals from our own perspectives, and because most products and their entrepreneurs are unique.
10. What are the 14 more common problems of in terms of marketing objectives?

    Target audience;

    Brand;

    Product;

    Platforms;

    Advertisements;

    Sales;

    Retention;

    Reach;

    Awareness;

ANSWERS

>Visibility;

>Accessibility;

>Frequency;

>Conversion; and,

>Distribution.

11. Are all ideas good?

    a. Yes.

12. Are all problems bad?

    a. Yes.

Chapter 7: Recap

1. Why are sales targets vital to campaign success?

    a. It gives you a definite goal to work towards and will help you to define your campaigns and their budgets.

2. How should you section your goals – daily, monthly, annually, or other?

    a. Ideally you should look at your target in terms of a 12-month financial goal. Divide this up into quarters, and months to get more real-time insight into whether or not you're reaching your target fast enough.

3. What is an opportunity?

    a. This is the overarching term encompassed of the opportunities you have to make a sale.

4. What is a general lead?

    a. These are the masses of leads that may come via your website or get in touch with you.

5. What is a marketing qualified lead?
   a. This are the leads that are ready to learn more about your brand and what you offer.
6. What are sales qualified leads?
   a. These are the leads that are ready to be sold on your products or services.
7. What is a healthy profit margin?
   a. 15%.
8. What is the average growth you can achieve for your website, year-on-year?
   a. 10%.
9. What are SMART goals?
   a. SMART stands for specific, measurable, attainable, relevant and time-bound.
10. What is retention?
    a. This is the rate at which you keep customers coming back to buy your products or services.
11. What is the best way to increase customer retention?
    a. The best way is to focus on customer satisfaction.
12. Where can you conduct affordable surveys?
    a. On social media platforms, such as Facebook.
13. What is up-selling?
    a. This is the process of offering a current 'sale' an add-on to their existing order.
14. How much of an ecommerce store's sales are generated by up-selling?
    a. Up to 30%.

ANSWERS

15. What is cross-selling?

    a. Cross-selling is the process of offering existing customers the first preference on new products or services.

16. How much do cross sales account for in total revenue?

    a. Up to 10%.

Chapter 8: Recap

1. What is a SWOT analysis?

    a. This is an analysis based on your brand's strengths, weaknesses, market opportunities, and threats.

2. What are marketing strengths?

    a. The general marketing resources that you have at your disposal.

3. What are marketing weaknesses?

    a. The general marketing resources that you don't have at your disposal.

4. What are marketing threats?

    a. The conditions that might hinder you from reaching your marketing objective.

5. What are marketing opportunities?

    a. Relevant industry trends that you can capitalize on.

6. How can you use this to address your marketing failures?

    a. Take on a marketing approach to your SWOT analysis in order to benchmark yourself against the competition and come up with industry-relevant solutions.

7. Why do you need to have different strategies for each goal?

   a. Your messaging and your promotions are going to be different depending on what you're trying to achieve. You can't just have the same approach to every single strategy, because their outcomes are going to be different, and thus the methods will need to be different too.

Chapter 9: Recap

1. Why do businesses with great products fail to pull in the numbers?

   a. Most of the time this is due to lack of marketing tactics.

2. What is the new 'cold-calling'?

   a. Marketing e-mails.

3. What is the gift you give to your customers when you engage in email marketing?

   a. You give them the gift of convenience. They can view it and answer it when they are ready to.

4. How should you personalize communiques?

   a. Use as much personal information as possible, such as the customers social standing and name. Speak to the categories that they fit into.

5. Is SMS marketing a cheaper alternative?

   a. No. It is more costly and your copy has to be on point.

6. Will content marketing be relevant in a post-pandemic world, and why?

    a. Absolutely. We are being preconditioned to interact with brands online, from the comforts of our homes.

7. What is affiliate marketing?

    a. This is the process of having a third-party re-seller with a good following in your niche, re-sell your products or services.

8. What is influencer marketing?

    a. This is the process of having a celebrity or social media influencer endorse your products or services.

9. What should you take into account before going about a video marketing campaign?

    a. Know your goal, where customers will be redirected to and develop a great call-to-action.

10. How can you increase your search rankings?

    a. Pose and answer as many questions as possible. Make sure to tap into social media to gain insight into what people are currently discussing.

11. What is pay-per-click marketing?

    a. This is a process of paying a nominal fee each time one of your ads are clicked.

12. How often should you check on your campaign progress?

    a. I would recommend that you check this daily. If you can't, then try to at least check in every three days.

Chapter 10: Recap

1. What is a sales deliverable?
   a. This refers to your actual delivery of a product or service.
2. What is a campaign deliverable?
   a. This refers to the timeline-bound deliverable, goal or sub-goal of a marketing campaign.
3. What should you create in order to keep upcoming campaigns on track?
   a. Create a campaign calendar and stick to it.
4. What steps can you take to make sure a product launch is on track?
   a. Find out how much time you need on a deliverable, keep everyone abreast of the roles they are playing, and prioritize the most important campaign factors as the ones which need first and major attention.

Chapter 11: Recap

1. What is ROI?
   a. This is your return on investment.
2. What is ROAS?
   a. This is your return on ad spend.
3. Can you factor in other gains, other than financial, into your ROI?
   a. Yes. The number of leads, new followers, post likes, and shares, amongst others, can be factored into your ROI.

ANSWERS

4. How do you work out your ROAS?

   a. This is worked out by dividing your campaign driven income by your expenditure.

5. What is EPROAS?

   a. Estimated profit return on ad spend.

6. What is the rule of thumb conversion rate for platforms like Facebook?

   a. As a rule of thumb use 1% for social media campaign conversion rates.

7. How do you work out your ROI?

   a. Simply. You subtract your expenditure from your campaign driven income.

8. What is cost-per-lead?

   a. According to your campaign expenditure and how much you gained in income, how much did each lead cost you.

9. How do you work out cost-per-lead?

   a. Campaign budget over total leads.

10. What is conversion rate?

    a. This refers to the number of leads you generate in comparison to the number of site visits.

11. How do you work out your conversion rate?

    a. Leads generated over number of visitors.

12. What is cost-per-sale?

    a. This is the comparison of your actual sales to your campaign budget.

13. How do you work out your cost-per-sale?

    a. Campaign budget over number of sales.

14. How do you work out your incremental sales?

    a. Campaign sales over monthly sales.

Chapter 12: Recap

1. What do you need to cultivate in terms of cash-flow early on?

    a. You need to cultivate the will power to say "no".

2. What are the key differences between spending money frivolously and spending money as an investment?

    a. When you spend to spend, your money is gone and doesn't return to you. When you spend to make, you are doing so with a strategy for it come back to you; quite possibly with interest.

3. What are 3 rules surrounding money mistakes?

    a. Rule #1 - Do not be afraid to make any money mistakes.

    Rule #2 - If you make a mistake, tell yourself "It's ok", try not to repeat it, and move on.

    Rule #3 - If you make the same mistake again, refer to Rule #2 and don't make a big fuss about it.

4. How can you control your cash flow?

    a. Find out your profitability;

    Draw up a cash flow projection; and,

    Speed up your income or inflows.

GLOSSARY

A/B Testing	This is the process of running two separate landing pages in accordance with two separate marketing campaigns in order to gauge which of the two is more effective.
Accessibility	This refers to how accessible your brand is for your target audience.
Advertisements	Advertisements include any public notice, announcement or promotion for your brand.
Affiliate marketing	Earning a or offering a commission based on secondary sales made by a third-party.
APAC region	Asia-Pacific Region.
Brand awareness	This refers to the level of awareness that the general public and your target audience have of your brand.
Brand Color Representation	This refers to the process of selecting colors to represent your brand which align with your brand message.
Brand Elements & Shapes	This refers to the all-encompassing elements of your brand and visual dynamics.
Brand Experience	This is the experience that customers and staff experience when they engage with your brand.

Brand Image & Positioning	This is what you create in order to solidify a certain image in the mind of your target market.
Brand Language & Tone	This is the recurrent language, phrases and manner of speaking that your brand uses to engage its target audience.
Brand name	This can be a trademarked name that represents your brand.
Brand Personality & Characteristics	These are the human traits which are attributed to your brand. It is how your target audience relates to your brand.
Brand Value Perception	This can often be measured by the price that your target audience is willing to pay for your product or services. It refers to the perceived value they gain from using your brand.
Brand	This is how you differentiate yourself from the competition.
Campaign goals	This addresses what you desire to achieve and what you need to change in order to do so.
Closing rate	This refers to the rate at which you are able to close sales in comparison to leads.
Competitor	This is a brand or business who bear similar resemblance to you in terms of offering and provide a product or service to customers in your target market.
Content marketing	This is the process of creating and distributing content of high quality and high value to your target market in order to win over following and loyalty.
Conversion	This is the rate at which you can turn a lead into a sale.
Customer acquisition	This is the process of bringing in new customers.

GLOSSARY

Customer retention	This is the process of retaining customers in order to continue selling products or services to them.
Customer	This is someone who actively purchases your products or services.
Digital marketing	This is the process of using internet-based tools and techniques to win over customers.
Distribution	This refers to how you are able to spread your products or services throughout the target market.
DRS	In our case, this refers to Data, reach and speed.
E-mail marketing	This involves acquiring personal contact information of potential and existing customers, and then marketing your current or new products and services to them.
Environment	This involves all of the prevailing internal and external factors which have an impact on your marketing and business operations.
FOMO	An acronym for the new age term, fear of missing out.
Frequency	This refers to how frequently you are able to reach your target market.
Gross profit	This is your overall profit.
Influencer marketing	This involves hiring the services of an influencer, often with a good presence on social media, who will endorse and promote your brand.
Lead generation	This refers to the process of acquiring potential customers or opportunities.
Lead nurturing	This is the process of developing a relationship with potential customers and converting them into an active customer.

Logo	This is a symbol or image which represents your brand.
Marketing qualified leads	These leads require further nurturing as they are not ready to be sold to yet.
Net profit	This is your remaining profit after expenditure.
Objectives	These define the goals that you set out in order to grow your revenue, and can include lead generation, targeting and retention, amongst others.
Place	This refers to the virtual or physical location where you will be selling your products or services.
Platforms	This refers to digital platforms where you might engage with your target audience.
Post engagement	This refers to how many likes, clicks, comments and shares your post gets.
PPC	This refers to pay-per-click advertising.
Price	This is the actual price which you sell your products and services for.
Product	This refers to a physical or virtual product that you sell.
Profit margin	This is the percentage of profit you make as a calculation based off of your overall revenue.
Promotion	This refers to how you go about promoting your brand, business, products or services.
Reach	This is the estimated number of people you can 'reach' with your marketing efforts.
Retention	This refers to the number of customers or rate at which you can retain existing customers.
Revenue	These are the fees earned for providing a product or service.
ROAS	This is return on ad spend.
ROI	This is return on investment.

Sales opportunities	This is a prospective customer who has some potential to be converted into a marketing qualified lead.
Sales qualified leads	These are the leads who are ready to move on to purchasing from you.
Sales	The number of monetary exchanges you make in return for products or services.
SEO	This is search engine optimization.
SMART goals	This is an acronym for Specific, Measurable, Attainable, Relevant and Tim-Based goals.
SMS marketing	Marketing via subscriber approved text messaging.
Social media marketing	Marketing via social media platforms such as Facebook, LinkedIn, Instagram and more.
SWOT analysis	This is an analysis based on your brand's strengths, weaknesses, opportunities and threats.
Tagline	A catchphrase or slogan that becomes synonymous with your brand.
Target audience	A particular group of prospective buyers which you target your products or services towards via the use of marketing campaigns.
Thought leadership	This is the process of showcasing your industry knowledge in order to come off as an authority in your field.
USP	This is your unique selling point; what makes you different from the competition.
Video marketing	This refers to a customer-facing marketing strategy through the use of video advertisements and campaigns.
Visibility	This refers to how visible your brand is within the market.
Web traffic	This refers to the amount of web visitors to your brand's website.

www.ingramcontent.com/pod-product-compliance
Lightning Source LLC
Chambersburg PA
CBHW052353220526

45465CB00003BA/1088